All The Things She Said

*Everything I know about modern
lesbian and bi culture*

Daisy Jones

CORONET

First published in Great Britain in 2021 by Coronet
An Imprint of Hodder & Stoughton
An Hachette UK company

1

Copyright © Daisy Jones 2021

A CIP catalogue record for this title is available from the British Library

Hardback ISBN 9781529328035
eBook ISBN 9781529328066

Typeset in Sabon MT by Hewer Text UK Ltd, Edinburgh
Printed and bound in Great Britain by Clays Ltd, Elcograf S.p.A.

Hodder & Stoughton policy is to use papers that are natural, renewable
and recyclable products and made from wood grown in sustainable
forests. The logging and manufacturing processes are expected to
conform to the environmental regulations of the country of origin.

Hodder & Stoughton Ltd
Carmelite House
50 Victoria Embankment
London EC4Y 0DZ

www.hodder.co.uk

A note on the text:

All pronouns used were what the interviewees asked me to use at the time of writing, but that may have changed since publication. Although I have endeavoured to make this book inclusive throughout, it has been written from my own limited perspective and I cannot claim to represent all lesbian/bi identities. Please refer to the final pages for a further reading list on books written about LGBTQ+ culture and queerness from other authors.

Contents

Preface

C lose your eyes and think of the word 'lesbian'. Roll it around on your tongue for a moment: L-E-S-B-I-A-N. What does the word conjure up? If you'd asked me that ten or fifteen years ago, a few things may have sprung to mind. Vegan lentil recipes and weird ethical sandals, perhaps. Hairy armpits and U-Hauled couples with their two cats, Kathleen and Hanna. Nut milks and moon cups and scissoring. Plaid shirts and IKEA trips and dungarees made from hemp. Basically, anything that sits at the other end of 'fun' and 'glamour' in the eyes of the mainstream. If gay men have historically been fetishised as flamboyant, fun-loving, promiscuous divas, lesbians are the opposite. We're the sexless killjoys of the LGBTQ party. The ones who'd rather stay at home building DIY shelves and organising our rune stones than, I don't know, going out and having fun. (Many of these stereotypes absolutely apply to me by the way, but only when I say so myself and only when they're celebrated).

Culture-wise, bi and pan women arguably have it even worse. Again, if you'd asked me what the word 'bisexual' conjured up a decade or so ago, I'd have probably thought about pornos and purple hair and Megan Fox's character in *Jennifer's Body*, the one where she plays a manipulative vampire with an unquench-able thirst for blood (iconic, yes, but hardly representative of bisexuals across the board.) Outside of that, bisexual women have been stereotyped as sex-obsessed and attention-seeking, confused and indecisive, even by lesbians themselves (*especially* by lesbians themselves). People have a hard time accepting that bisexual women, as an orientation, exist. According to mono-sexuals, they're either straight women who are drunk / 'having a bit of a moment' or else gay women only halfway out of the closet. To be bisexual is to be a human bridge, apparently.

Over the past few years, however, there's been a subtle yet tangible shift. One that's hard to pinpoint and even harder to describe. The culture of queer women is no longer, perhaps, some-thing to be whispered or winced at in public. The culture of queer women is everywhere. It's Kristen Stewart in a backwards cap sticking her middle finger up at the paps. It's Janelle Monáe show-ing up on the red carpet in assless chaps and a butt-length plait. It's Hunter Schafer and all her different coloured eyeshadows. It's slicked-back hair and cheekbones and vests and monochrome and popped collars. It's tarot cards and lunch dates with exes and shout-typing 'SPIT IN MY MOUTH' at any woman celeb pictured wearing a tailored tux. It's Whoopi Goldberg saying she's never loved any of her husbands. It's Justin Bieber getting married. It's Gillian Anderson playing a sex therapist. It's describing some-thing as 'really dykey' and feeling the spiky consonants sit satisfy-ingly in your mouth, because everyone wants to look dykey, don't they? To look 'dykey' is to wear cut-off denims and scuffed Vans while carrying a leather sex bench into the home you share with your lover, like Cara Delevingne and Ashley Benson. To look 'dykey' is to look like you know what to do with your hands.

None of this is to say that the culture of queer women *itself* has improved or expanded or 'turned cool', or whatever. Lesbian and bi culture has always existed. We've always been stylish and horny and campy in our own ways, long before this generation of queers and the generations before them existed. No, the shift exists in the way lesbian and bi culture is beginning to trickle into the mainstream, now so more than ever. Our inner language, our lowkey signifiers, our private way of being is – to some degree, although not completely – being pushed out into the wider public sphere. Our identities are now often esteemed as much as they were once disparaged. As the lesbian culture writer Jill Gutowitz told *Buzzfeed* in 2019: 'If I had been tweeting about how hot Miley Cyrus was in 2009, my friends would've been like, "Ew, you fucking dyke!" and I would've deleted it and cried. Now that we're allowed to talk about it publicly and have thousands of other people on Twitter agree with us, the thirst is pouring out of us in these violent outbursts.'

This is an era in which queer women are helping to shape modern pop culture – just as they always have done. If gay men and drag queens can in a roundabout way be credited with the current Kardashian aesthetic – hyper femininity, big hair, arched eyebrows – queer women can be seen as the ones injecting a campy butchness, a queer sensibility, a certain dykey vibe into pop culture's lexicon. Just take a look at Samira Wiley on the cover of *Stylist*, hair shaved, fresh turtleneck, eyes raised to meet yours. Take a look at Rachel Weisz striding towards Olivia Colman before choking her against the bedpost in *The Favourite*. Pay close attention to Zendaya, slumped over and staring mood- ily from beneath a burgundy hoodie in *Euphoria*. We might even say that some of the most lusted after poster boys of this gener- ation – Harry Styles, Timothée Chalamet, Justin Bieber – take cues from the style and substance of queer women. Lean in a little closer, and these floppy-haired, cheek-boned cis men start to look remarkably like soft butches. As queer scholar and activist Marie Cartier pointed out way back in 2003: 'A traditional stereotype of butch women is that they are acting like men — I think the opposite is the case. It is the New Man, which emerged after the Second World War, who acts like a woman — a butch woman.'

I wrote this book in part because I'm interested in how this shift occurred. How lesbian and bi culture (which can be viewed as two separate things, while also being inextricably interlinked) went from something coded and covert and word-of-mouth to something we see on the red carpet, on *Buzzfeed* listicles, smattered across our iPhone screens and timelines and in magazines. How lesbian and bi culture went from being the butt of everyone's joke (even within the gay community), to all your straight mates suddenly cutting in homemade mullets and wearing thumb rings and calling Meryl Streep 'Daddy'. How lesbian and bi culture went from being something you associate with those two middle-aged 'aunts' in your mum's village with the spiked frosted tips, to having screenwriter Lena Waithe grace the cover of *Vanity Fair* in a white tee and chain, shoulders hunched and casual, eyes staring straight into the camera with what I can only describe as a 'powerful lesbian expression'. Maybe even more than that, I wanted to try to get to the heart of what it means to be lesbian or bi today, culturally. As a teenager, I pored over whatever queer stuff I could get hold of. Marvelled at *Paris Is Burning*. Savoured the taste of Susan Sontag's seminal text *Notes on Camp*. Cackled out loud during hungover mornings watching *Party Monster*. Spent my uni years having strong emotions about each and every contestant on *RuPaul's Drag Race*. But these brilliant, sparkling portals into LGBTQ culture were, more often than not, focused on men. The culture of queer women has always been harder to access; required a heavier dose of effort and detective work and reading between the lines. The texts I did come across about queer women were often hefty academic things, or based in a kind of classic American conservative lesbiandom that felt quite distant from my own.

Of course, just because lesbian and bi culture has always been rare to see in the mainstream doesn't mean that it has ever been flimsy or insubstantial. As with all queer communities, the culture of queer women was born on the ground – out of clubs and codes and social circles. I learned more about queer culture from stumbling into an East End gay bar – surrounded by girls with septum rings, girls with their limbs propped up in right angles at the bar, girls staring daggers at their exes' new lovers – than I did from anything I saw on TV or at the cinema. These spaces were integral: they offered escapism and communality in real, physical ways, separate from the outside world. Outside of clubbing, it was about what friends were into, the way they'd dress, the things we'd say to each other. Later, it was how we existed online. Either way, wherever that space was forged – online, offline, in the club or out of the club – the culture always came from queer people, it was always moulded in our form.

When pop culture gets it right, then, it acts as a mirror being held up to a queer reality cultivated on the ground. We don't love Robyn's 'Dancing On My Own' just because we collectively decided to. We love it because it feels familiar. We love it because it's steely and glittering and imbued with a kind of euphoria and unrequited longing that we recognise in ourselves, as queer people. 'Dancing On My Own' is the sound of queerness, not the other way round. You could say the same thing about much of queer culture.

My life would end up being shaped and ultimately changed by the culture of queer women. As a kid I dressed like a soft butch baby-dyke – 'boy's' jeans, big T-shirts, jagged dark hair like Mowgli. I liked playing football, skateboarding, swapping

Pokémon cards, kicking around abandoned houses. My friends and I would race down hills and spray Lynx cans at lighter flames and break into school at the weekends so that we could kickflip down the smooth cement steps that poured across the playground like charcoal liquid. I was, to all intents and purposes, a 'tomboy', though I bristled at the label myself. I hadn't yet stepped into my queerness, maybe hadn't even recognised it, but I knew that the way I held myself, the way I existed in my body, the way I related to other genders, had an oddness about it in comparison to a lot of other girls my age.

As is the case with so many of us, this oddness was quickly flattened out of me once I reached my teenage years and had to swallow an alarming dose of compulsory heterosexuality. I speak more on this later in the book, but I think there's a time in your life – thirteen, fourteen – when the world-at-large starts to really hammer down on the idea that you need to be desirable; your value as a person becomes based on your attractiveness to the opposite sex, specifically. This might not be the 1950s anymore, but to be a palatable woman is still to be femme, submissive and to adhere to a certain version of the male gaze. I grew my hair out then, shoved myself awkwardly into push-up bras and figure-strangling dresses, nursed crushes on boys because that's what teenage girls are supposed to do, right before we find a man who wants to keep us and marry us and raise healthy, bouncing, heterosexual children of our own.

Discovering and immersing myself in lesbian and bi culture in my early twenties, then, was like going back to how I was when I was a kid, back before I became encumbered with what I was 'supposed' to be like. There's an authenticity that sits right at the heart of queer culture that makes it inherently appealing. The things that society teaches you to hate about yourself – the way you cross your legs on a chair, the way T-shirts hang on your body, the stuff that holds your attention – queer culture more readily embraces. Within the culture of lesbians especially, the male gaze – the idea that you should dress and act a certain way to appease men – is taken out almost entirely. It's simply not there. And what you have left is space, endless free space to be yourself. Without sounding sickeningly sincere, when I found queer culture I definitely found myself again.

This book, then, is a love letter of sorts to the modern culture of queer women and – where relevant – non-binary people (I mention non-binary people here and in instances throughout because, as I explore later on in the book, non-binary lesbians exist, as do non-binary bi folk, as do non-binary people who partly – although not completely – identify with aspects of womanhood or dykeness). This is not an academic rehashing of the past. I'm not a historian or theorist – there are plenty of bold, in-depth queer history books out there already, many of which I have listed at the end of this book. It's also not the whole jigsaw, but more like a piece of it. Because when it comes to lesbian and bi culture, there has never been one singular narrative, in the same way that not all straight people like to drink WKD or get married by thirty or have strong feelings about Paul Mescal and Adam Driver. My experience is UK based: I grew up in east London, spent almost my whole life here. I'm also in my twenties, at a very specific time in history, meaning a lot of the interviews and references in this book reflect the time and location I'm coming from. My understanding of queer culture is going be very different to that of the next person, and very different to that of those who came before me.

With that in mind, this can be viewed as my contribution. This is everything I've learned as a queer woman about queer culture. Everything that others have taught me. The world of nightlife. Our pop music. Our style and signifiers. How we've been represented on TV and in film. How we gather online. What it's like to date as a lesbian or bisexual person. What it's like to lose your mind. What being a 'lesbian' or 'queer' or 'bi' even means right now, at a time when ideas about gender and identity and intimacy are loosening up and expanding; how queer culture fits into that, how any of us manage to fit into anything and whether we even want to.

I spoke to countless lesbian and bi people for this book, young and old, heard their stories and gathered their perspectives. They told me their versions of romance. They told me their versions of style. How they came out and how they learned to express themselves. How their queerness was a gift, then a curse, then a gift again. Each and every story diverges and overlaps somehow, including my own; some of them contradict each other. This is my attempt to sew the whole thing together.

CHAPTER ONE

What is a Lesbian Anyway?

Just off the Turkish coast, in the north-eastern Aegean Sea, lies the Greek island of Lesbos. It's a huge, triangular island, crammed full with olive groves, fruit trees and Mediterranean pines that cover the mountainous land like a blanket. Locals have been known to refer to the place as 'Emerald Island' because it glistens green, always bursting with life; unusual for an island of its mammoth size and hot temperature. But Lesbos isn't just known for its flora and sunshine. It's also known for being the reason the word 'lesbian' became a term to describe gay women.

It makes sense that the word would have derived from an island such as Lesbos; a place brimming in wildlife and intense volcanic activity, yet completely isolated from the mainland. What could be more lesbian than that? But the etymology has more to do with one of the island's most ancient inhabitants, the Greek poet Sappho, who is said to have spent her life (c. 630BC. 570 BC) writing lines and lines of gorgeous stanzas about women, love, anguish and desire.

Much of Sappho's poetry has been lost or heavily retranslated. Her sexuality has also long been up for debate (you can imagine the centuries-long line of classicists desperately trying to find evidence against one of the most influential and esteemed poets being a massive dyke). But regardless of what we know or don't know about Sappho, the flagrant homoeroticism of her poetry opens itself up like a flower, constantly. 'Sappho 31' is one of her most famous fragments. It's incomplete, and has been through endless translations, but the story it tells is as old as unrequited lesbian love itself. It basically shares the same plot as the TV drama *Sugar Rush*.

> *He seems to me an equal of the gods—*
> *whoever gets to sit across from you*
> *and listen to the sound of your sweet speech*
> > *so close to him,*

> *to your beguiling laughter: O it makes my*
> *panicked heart go fluttering in my chest,*
> *for the moment I catch sight of you there's no*
> > *speech left in me,*

> *but tongue gags—: all at once a faint*
> *fever courses down beneath the skin,*
> *eyes no longer capable of sight, a thrum-*
> > *ming in the ears,*

> *and sweat drips down my body, and the shakes*
> *lay siege to me all over, and I'm greener*
> *than grass, I'm just a little short of dying,*
> > *I seem to me;*

> *but all must be endured, since even a pauper . . .*

Despite Sappho's poetry being older than Christ, 'lesbian' – as a broad descriptor of female homosexuality – didn't become a word we used in the UK until around the late nineteenth century, when European sexologists began acknowledging that same-sex attraction and practices between women did in fact exist. To them, the term 'lesbian' was used to describe what they considered a pathological abnormality, a biological anomaly, a sort of insanity. To be a lesbian meant that you were 'inverted', that you wished to be a man and that you envied their penises. And the only cure for this terrible affliction, they thought, was to settle down and marry a man, immediately, dedicating yourself to a more 'practical' lifestyle involving breastmilk and housework.

Equating lesbianism with insanity sounds absurd and offensive to us now. But before then, the idea that women might be into women was pretty much never spoken out loud. (It's worth pointing out here that while gay men were routinely persecuted for 'sodomy', sexual activity between women was rarely acknowledged because female pleasure as an end in itself wasn't acknowledged either. In 1811, for example, two Scottish schoolmistresses ended up in court after being accused of repeatedly going at it in the boarding-school bed. One of the judges hearing the case, Lord Meadowbank, claimed that sex between women was 'equally imaginary with witchcraft, sorcery or carnal copulation with the devil' and the girls were promptly acquitted. They were just giving each other massages, he shrugged, and everyone agreed.)

Using the word 'lesbian' to describe a form of sexual deviancy or abnormality, then, established lesbians as a) existing, and b) outsiders, which inadvertently made way for the beginnings of lesbian subculture. In other words, the label 'lesbian', however derogatory, positioned lesbians as being part of a social identity as well as a so-called medical one. In her 1999 book *Encyclopedia of Lesbian Histories and Cultures*, lesbian theorist Bonnie Zimmerman explains it like this: 'The lesbian label made it possible to define a relationship between women as explicitly sexual, and, as such, the label was welcomed by some women in spite of the stigma attached to it. The lesbian communities, cultures, and, eventually, social movements that have grown over the course of the twentieth century have been built upon the very lesbian label that originated as a stigma.'

Fast forward to the 1960s and 1970s, when gay rights movements were really hitting their stride across the UK, Europe and US especially, and the word 'lesbian' had transformed into something else entirely. It was no longer a medical term solely used to describe women who had sex with other women and were therefore mentally ill. There were people who still believed that of course – people who still do – but 'lesbian' was an identity, a label embraced by gay women and worn with pride. Lesbians formed organisations and developed political ideologies addressing their needs. They wore T-shirts emblazoned with 'Nobody knows I'm a lesbian' and waved flags that read, 'A day without lesbians is like a day without sunshine'. They marched alongside gay men, transgender people and genderqueer folk for equal rights. All of which is to say: the word 'lesbian' was no longer simply a catch-all phrase for women who were into women. It was considered by many to be an identity, too, as well as an orientation.

It didn't take long for the term to become loaded with political meaning; electrons of an atom darting in all sorts of directions. By the 1970s and 1980s, a lot of lesbians had become dissatisfied with their exclusion from both feminist spaces and gay liberation organisations. Radical lesbian feminists sought to separate themselves from both of these groups, viewing any tie to the patriarchy, and by extension heterosexuality, as oppressive. Some set up communes, 'womyn only' music festivals, bought acres of land in which to live separately from men and straight people. The intention was to entirely reject both mainstream society and the activist circles that had invisiblised them. I mention all of this not to rehash a history lesson, but to explain the ways in which the word 'lesbian' had become more than just a descriptor. It was synonymous with a variety of ideals. It was a way of life.

The idea of a lesbian-only utopia where a bunch of women are growing courgettes all day and going down on each other all night might sound kind of idyllic on the surface. But the tenants of these certain strands of lesbian feminism – mainly among the white and middle class – looked to many a little outdated and exclusionary. Bisexuality was routinely scorned or outright denied (if you were going near penises you were liaising with the enemy!). Transgender women were regularly misgendered and excluded from lesbian feminist circles. Sex work, kink and pornography were considered anti-feminist, patriarchal, violent. Butch–femme identities were maligned as nothing more than heterosexist role-play. Lesbians of colour and working-class lesbians, too, often felt just as sidelined within certain lesbian feminist circles as they were in feminist and gay ones. (You can hear this frustration pour out in Audre Lorde's open letter to the 'radical' white lesbian feminist Mary Daly, in 1979: 'To dismiss our Black foremothers may well be to dismiss where European women learned to love. As an African-American woman in white patriarchy, I am used to having my archetypal experience distorted and trivialised, but it is terribly painful to feel it being done by a woman whose knowledge so much touches my own.')

For many, such essentialist ideas about gender and sexuality simply didn't feel right. More than that: it felt actively invisibling. Gender could be playful, pliable – couldn't it? Sexuality could be fluid, fragmented. Maybe you were in love with the person, not the uterus. Maybe you didn't feel like a woman *or* a man. Maybe being submissive and kinky made you feel powerful and connected to your partner. Maybe it turned you on. For a lot of people, lesbian feminism may have laid some important groundwork, but the more rigid facets of the movement didn't chime with everyone. It didn't seem to make way for all the colour and complexities of gender and desire. Younger generations in the 1990s turned to queer theory. They pored over *How to Bring Your Kids Up Gay* by Eve Sedgwick (1989) and *Gender Trouble* by Judith Butler (1990) and *Fear of a Queer Planet* by Michael Warner (1993) and *Female Masculinity* by Jack Halberstam (1998). They embraced the idea that you didn't have to be one thing, you could be many, or nothing definitive at all. Queer theory didn't cancel out lesbianism as a concept. Instead it made way for the word 'lesbian' to be viewed from different angles, like a placeholder. There isn't one way to be lesbian, said the queer theorists, just as there isn't one way to be queer.

Today, the word 'lesbian' remains complex, fluctuating and constantly up for debate. Ask a random person on the street what the word 'lesbian' means and they'll probably tell you that it's a term to describe women who are exclusively into women. That's the straightforward consensus. But lesbianism is harder to define when you call into question ideas about gender, intimacy and identity, and how those three things intertwine and mutate. I have called myself lots of things over the years: queer, bisexual, pansexual, gay, lesbian, dyke. My most recent and snug fitting has been 'pansexual homoromantic' (accurate for me right now, even though it does sound like a type of forklift truck). But often I feel like all of the aforementioned at once. When I call myself a lesbian it's because the majority of my most meaningful romantic and sexual encounters have been with women, and I surround myself with lesbian culture and queer women. But I also fancy men occasionally. I watch porn involving men, too. When I use a strap-on, it turns me on to imagine that it is part of my body, that I am penetrating my partner with a penis that belongs to me. When my partner uses a strap-on, it turns me on to imagine the other way round. Sometimes, I feel attracted to something that seems to exist outside of gender entirely, or at least in some sort of grey area. The way David Bowie laughs lightly, knowingly, in the third verse of 'Starman'. The soft arrogance of a near-stranger winking at me from across a room. The vision of my girlfriend getting dressed in the morning, the way her body stoops into boxers and jeans, blond hair awry in the window-sun, like some sort of cherubic twink. None of this feels attached to gender. Does that make me any less of a lesbian? I don't think so. But it does highlight the limits of language and labels when it comes to our identities. Or at least the necessity of recognising words as umbrellas rather than boxes.

To that end, there will be others who share the same sexuality/gender 'make-up' as myself who prefer to call themselves bi or pan. There will be others who lean more towards sleeping with or loving men who also call themselves bi or pan. Others might not subscribe to anything at all, or prefer the ambiguity of being 'sexually fluid'. Again, words are less about attaching exact, specific labels to a person's desires and more about however that person feels comfortable expressing them. For a long time, for instance, a lot of bisexual people shunned the term because it was assumed that 'bi' meant being into only men or women, which many viewed as compounding a gender binary. These days, however, 'bi' is more accurately understood as being into 'your own gender and other people's.' It's not the words or desires that have changed; it's our understanding of them.

Our collective conception of lesbianism and bisexuality has updated along with our conception of womanhood and gender. Trans people, for instance, disrupt outdated notions of both of those things. Trans people have existed for as long as humanity itself. (There are Sumerian and Akkadian texts dating as far back as 4,500 years ago that document trans people, while some North American indigenous cultures have always recognised 'third genders' or multi-genders, among a few examples.) Meaning that trans lesbians have also existed for as long as time. But there are still trans-exclusionary 'radical' feminists in mainstream public discourse today who deny the existence of trans women and therefore deny the existence of trans lesbians. To them then, the word 'lesbian' is reduced to nothing but biology and genitals and chromosomes. But this doesn't sit accurately with a lot of cisgender lesbians either, let alone trans lesbians. I am a lesbian because I feel like one – not because I have a vagina and my fingers have been inside someone else's. Even if those things weren't true, I would still be a lesbian. And while feminism's second wave can be viewed as significant, culture-shifting, trans-exclusionary rhetorics like the above not only actively isolate and therefore endanger trans people, but they also erase the very fundamental role that trans people play – and have always played – in lesbian culture and queer liberation more generally.

Alice is slight and Scottish and speaks so softly that I have to tell her to shout down the receiver. She wears turtlenecks and glasses, tailored suits and matching eyeshadow and has 'too cute to be cis' written wryly in her Instagram bio. She tells me that the word 'lesbian' has often felt kind of loaded to her for a lot of reasons. Coming out, for her, had to happen twice. Five years ago, at seventeen, she came out as trans, which was no easy feat, especially not in the small working-class area of Glasgow where she grew up, in which queers 'would always be the punchline of a joke'. Her 'trans awakening' of sorts came after watching *My Transsexual Summer*, a 2011 documentary on Channel 4 about seven trans people at different stages of their transition. Something about it rang deep and true and a lot of old feelings clicked into place. 'I'd never met a trans person or seen a trans person until watching that show.'

What followed were weeks of late-night Google searches for terms like 'gender dysphoria', before erasing the browsing history on the family computer. It wasn't that she hadn't before *felt* like the woman she was, but that she hadn't yet encountered the language to explain it. Now she had. Alice tells me she feels strongly about people being given the words in which to articulate their experiences and understand themselves for this reason. The alternative – in which trans understanding is in the shadows, pushed underground, misrepresented – can be deeply oppressive, damaging to the psyche. For Alice, LGBTQ education has always been a political issue as well as a psychological one. 'It was the same with Section 28,' she says 'The Tories didn't want to teach people about being gay because they didn't want people to be gay, essentially. It's the same shit now.'.

Coming out as a lesbian two years later was both simpler and more complicated. Before transitioning, Alice had tried and pretty much failed to be attracted to men (a lesbian story as old as time). But back then, the idea of being with a woman when she was still presenting as a cis man didn't make her feel happy either. Especially when 'womanhood' is so culturally intertwined with having sex with men, thanks to compulsory heterosexuality. She tries to explain her old mindset by using her reaction to the famous trans YouTuber Gigi Gorgeous as an example: 'I think she came out as a lesbian. She has a female partner now. And I remember being so young and stupid at the time that I got annoyed with her. For some reason I thought "Oh cis people will just think that trans people are unsure of their gender identity and are mixing and matching." I didn't even understand the difference between sexuality and gender. I think a lot of people still don't. They get the two really conflated.'

Once again it was a TV show that caused the penny to drop. *First Dates* this time, also on Channel 4. There were two women going on a date, sharing food, flirting easily. They seemed so free, so beautiful. Alice realised that she was looking at something she wanted. More than wanted. Something that fit. 'So, I then went onto Tinder and put my settings onto "woman" and after that I have never turned back. I've been a massive fucking dyke ever since,' she laughs. 'I never did a big coming out like "I'm a lesbian". I just brought a girl home to my mum. I said to her, "Mum, I'm going to bring my partner home, she happens to be a girl", and she was totally fine with it.'

Talking to Alice about lesbianism is enlightening. We speak at length about the weight behind the term, its history, how you can identify as being a lesbian while still being afraid to utter the word with confidence. This rings twice as true for trans women. 'I sometimes still feel like I can't classify myself as a "lesbian" because there are so many people out there who fundamentally disagree with that. So I do it more for myself. I would just say I'm "queer" to my friends, if that makes any sense. I really would love to call myself a lesbian with confidence, but there's something about the word that I feel like kind of excludes me. I worry about upsetting others, more than anything, and I don't want to be someone who makes anyone unhappy, which is probably my fucking problem.'

Alice identifies with the word 'lesbian' because – like a lot of lesbians – she's never really been attracted to men, physically or emotionally. It's that simple. Even so, lesbian-only spaces haven't always felt like safe spaces. 'I probably would now feel a lot more accepted into lesbian spaces, possibly since having SRS [sex reassignment surgery]. I don't know why, but I would personally feel more comfortable and confident in myself if I had a cisgender body of a woman. But I have joined a lesbian book club before and that was really sweet. Twitter sometimes feels like a safe space too if you follow the right people. And queer clubs like Dalston Superstore [in London], where you know you're not really going to get any hassle from anyone for being yourself. You can be as dykey as you want, go in wearing assless chaps, whatever.'

Once we reject reductive, sex-based ideas about gender, lesbians are just women who are mostly intimate with other women, right? But it's not just women who identify as being lesbian. A lot of people today are recognising gender and sexuality, and the link between them, as constantly fluctuating and multitudinous.

A, twenty-three, has a feathery mullet and round, cartoonish glasses. They skate in their spare time, and dance, and grow plants. They're also a non-binary lesbian. For a long time they delayed coming out as non-binary because they thought it meant they wouldn't be a lesbian anymore, or that their experience would somehow be erased. 'That made me very uncomfortable,' they explain. 'I guess I thought lesbianism was a connection between women, and being trans would strip me of the community I'd found and the understanding I had of my sexuality that had taken so long to get to. It took me slowly internalising that gender and sexuality are not binary and in fact are a spectrum. Meeting other non-binary lesbians and discussing these intersections made me feel comfortable in my identity.'

The idea that lesbians needn't always be women might sound strange to the straight mainstream or those who subscribe to more dominant, binary ideas about gender and sexuality (ideas that can be widely understood as the result of European colonialism, rather than intrinsic). To A though, it's pretty simple. Words are just placeholders for complex human experiences after all. And words evolve, bend into new shapes, adapt. (It's worth pointing out here, too, that 'non-binary' is an all-encompassing term for those who do not fully and exclusively identify as male or female. Where a non-binary person exists on that spectrum will entirely depend on the person.) A explains: 'Because most of our language is built around binary ideas of gender and sexuality, I don't feel like there is the language to describe the complex experiences of queerness. So, we use existing language to try to communicate best how we really feel.' What does the word 'lesbian' mean to them personally?

'I now feel that lesbianism is partially about who I find I'm attracted to (mostly people who are also lesbians) and partly about finding a community of people with a shared history, experiences and culture.'

A uses the word 'lesbian' because it still describes their sexuality, separate to their gender. But a lot of non-binary people and trans men who once used the word no longer feel it fits. Franx, a twenty-eight-year-old trans guy, remembers calling himself a lesbian back when he was a teenager. Not because he only fancied girls – he 'really, really fancied guys too' – but because it was almost a way to express his masculinity, to describe the culture he'd become immersed in. 'Bisexual' just didn't seem to pack the same punch. 'I felt extremely masculine. I felt like I needed a different way to express that verbally, so the word "lesbian" was a rebellion, a way to disrupt conversation. When I was a teenager, I was at a house party, and a boy came up and said "I wouldn't go near you with a ten-foot barge pole" and I was like, "Well, I'm a lesbian."'

But 'lesbian' didn't fit either, not properly. Nothing did but everything did at the same time. He left his small town on the outskirts of Nottingham, moved to Brighton to study Fine Art Painting, became intrigued and interested in ideas about gender and body parts and what any of it meant or didn't mean or could. 'I used to say I was a gay man trapped in a lesbian's body at the time,' he remembers. 'I didn't realise that I was a trans guy. I was very reticent to commit to a solid word. I started just not liking words, because they felt too restrictive. Then when I finally came out as trans, when I was twenty-five or something, I had a psychotic episode.' He ended up in a psychiatric ward for a few weeks, an experience he describes as a 'culmination of all of this repressed reality of my transness. It's been a really complex journey. I've identified as a lot of things.'

These days Franx has 'post-verbal' stick 'n' poked on his body. He uses minoxidil to grow a moustache. He expresses his masculinity while also keeping one critical eye hovering above gender at all times, just as he always has. 'Trying to pin down gender and what it is is impossible,' he laughs. 'It's been conceptualised in infinite different ways throughout history by different cultures and different people and they're all valid. But you've got to have something to work with, to try and work yourself out. To work on pure concept without context is like . . . where the fuck are you? That's what caused my psychotic episode. There was no context to what I knew about gender. I knew too fucking much about gender and how that had been expressed, and it was hard to pinpoint where I sat within that. I'm just trying to keep it simple at the moment.'

Franx is right, of course. Gender is a mindfuck. So is the word 'lesbian', and any of the placeholders we use to understand ourselves. But lesbianism gets more complicated still, when we take a deeper look at intimacy, and what that even means. When does something tip over from platonic to romantic, or sexual? And what about the many grey areas in between? When exactly do we slot the word 'lesbian' into this whole blurry miasma?

Before lesbian became a term to describe a type of sexual

(then considered deviant) relationship, 'non-sexual' romance between women was commonplace. Deep intimacy was expected among two female friends, sensuality encouraged. Take a look at the oil paintings of Jean Alphonse Roehn (1799–1864), in which women drape over each other in rumpled sheets, breasts exposed. See how one woman gazes longingly at another, rosy cheeked, in François Boucher's 1750 painting *The Love Letter*. To us today, these paintings look exceptionally dykey. Back then, they looked like platonic romance, nothing shiftier. Zimmerman explains: 'Historical studies demonstrate that, in the European and US middle and upper classes, intense, loving, exclusive relationships between women, termed "romantic friendships", were not only acceptable but honourable prior to the late nineteenth and early twentieth centuries. At that time, such relationships came to be seen as lesbian and deviant, and, eventually, the once widespread practice of romantic friendship became virtually extinct.'

You might take a look at a non-sexual relationship between women and say, 'That's not a lesbian relationship then.' But here's the catch: lesbians are still lesbians without the sex. Our understanding in that regard has evolved beyond that of before the nineteenth century. Some lesbians never have sex. Some lesbians never want it. Some lesbians have differing ideas about what sex means. When I look back on certain lesbian crushes, sex was sometimes not even part of the equation. I'd imagine what it was like to be close to them, to breathe in the same air they were breathing out, for them to secretly prefer me and my mind above all other people and their minds. I'd imagine a woman confiding in me. 'I need to tell you something,' she would say, gripping my hands in hers, eyes searching mine, maybe leading me into an empty classroom or side street (I'm not fussed). 'Something I've never told anybody.' *What, what is it?* I would whisper, my breath even, heart pounding. Then she would tell me about a murder, or a secret child, or the fact she could move things with her eyes without touching them, like Matilda. Whatever. It didn't matter. The point was that we shared a special bond now. Maybe we would kiss, but we didn't have to. Romantic intimacy needn't involve physical touch.

These romantic fantasies were very different to the ones I had about men, which would often involve sex with semi-faceless bodies, the more generic the better. This might sound cold and dead-eyed, but that's just me: I have not often experienced deep romantic feelings towards men. Those I slept with IRL probably thought I was a sociopath. 'Shall I make us some breakfast?' asked one especially gentle guy when I was at uni. He had a Welsh accent and wore a T-shirt that read 'NHS' above the shape of a Nike logo. We'd spent the previous night screaming along to Pavement beside my CD player, then we'd drunkenly read each other's poetry out loud, then at some point we'd ended up sleeping together. Breakfast, though? The intimacy made me uncomfortable. I told him I had to leave. None of this is to say that I could never fall in love with a man – of course I could, life knocks you sideways continuously – but it doesn't fit snugly like a glove in the way it sometimes does with women. For me, then, it's not sexual attraction that makes me a lesbian right now: it's romantic love. For others, it might be the other way around, or both. For many bisexual people, it might be more about the variant or combination. The way queer people express the many complexities of desire consistently varies.

The difference between romantic and sexual attraction is much discussed within asexual and aromantic communities. They call it the 'split attraction model', meaning that sexual and romantic orientation are two separate things and you might define yourself somewhere within those two spectrums. Bisexual biromantic. Lesbian aromantic. Heterosexual homoromantic. Homosexual biromantic. Pansexual homoromantic. Heteroromantic greysexual. The list goes on. I mention this in order to underline that the word 'lesbian' needn't be confined to sexual practice, or even sexual attraction without the sex. Lesbian asexuals exist, as do lesbian aromantics. In fact, there are quite a lot of them. There are even a group of people who define themselves as quoiromantics, which originates from the word '*quoi*,' meaning 'what' in French. Quoiromantics disidentify with the concept of romantic orientation altogether, or else constantly question the meaning of romance, perhaps not seeing a clear line between romance and friendship and other types of intimacy. Everything becomes blurred.

I manage to get in touch with a few asexual lesbians online. Charlotte, who asked me to change her name because she's not out to anybody other than close friends, was raised in a wealthy, conservative part of England. Like a lot of us, she grew up under the impression that 'lesbian' was a dirty word, only used as an insult. She recalls how the only out lesbian at school was constantly picked on. When another girl complained that she didn't want to get changed for PE in front of 'the lesbian', their teacher didn't call her out for being homophobic. Instead, she assured her that she could get changed elsewhere if it made her more comfortable. It would take Charlotte years to realise that the fact she wasn't even slightly interested in men, only women, probably meant that she was a lesbian too.

Recognising her own asexuality was a little more complicated. She knew that she was romantically interested in women, but why wasn't she *physically* attracted to anyone? Like Alice, she hadn't been given the language to explain it. 'People have said, like, "Oh you've just not met the right person yet", but I'm not really attracted to anybody in that sense,' she says. 'It's like something in my brain just doesn't exist. I've been seeing a psychotherapist and she was like, "You can be attracted to someone in an emotional sense, but it not go any further than that."

But I had just had no idea. Then I was like, "Oh yeah, that's what it is. I want to be with someone, but in an emotional way." ' For a while, Charlotte questioned whether this meant she wasn't a lesbian after all, but the more she learned about asexuality, the more she realised that sex needn't be the epicentre of her identity.

I find it especially interesting chatting to Charlotte about what it means to be romantic without physical intimacy, how a romantic relationship can differ from a close platonic friendship. For Charlotte, it's to do with deep connection and exclusivity. 'I think when you can share the deepest darkest depths of your mind, I suppose,' she says. 'I myself would define a romantic relationship as me and one other person, and they're the only person that I have that emotional connection with, and I'm the only person that they have that emotional connection with. Maybe it is a grey area when it's void of physical aspects, but if I considered myself "with" someone and then they slept with someone else, I would be devastated, even though I wouldn't want to do that. It's difficult.'

Other asexual lesbians, like Briana, who also asked me to change her name for privacy, have a less monogamous attitude towards relationships. They don't have strong feelings about sex, full stop. 'I don't mind them having sex with other people, but I don't want them to have sex with me. So that's a conversation that has to happen,' she explains down the phone, flipping the script on what we're used to hearing. 'I would much prefer to date somebody else who is asexual, but it's like trying to find a needle in a haystack. I'd probably be comfortable as part of a poly relationship as well. I'd be fine with that because an asexual being with someone who's very sexual wouldn't work necessarily? It's complicated. Relationship politics are complicated.'

Briana's coming out journey isn't dissimilar to Charlotte's. She too realised she was a lesbian before she realised she was asexual. When all of her friends were texting the numbers printed in teen magazines to get the latest screen wallpaper of some fit, oiled boy-bander for their Nokia phones, Briana wasn't interested. She wasn't attracted to men. It was women she was more interested in getting to know. So she first toyed with the idea of being bisexual. Then she came out as gay.

A few years ago, though, Briana began to get 'suspicious of herself'. She realised she didn't like having sex. She didn't even like kissing; she thought it was 'deeply unpleasant'. The way people stuck their tongues in each other's mouths, swirled them around, wanted to get up close and personal. Dates often culminated in the expectation that they would kiss, which was a problem. 'I never realised that it was an unusual thing, I guess? It's not something I was talking about with my friends, because I was still trying hard to keep it a secret,' she says.

'Once I started thinking about it, I thought, I don't enjoy having sex with people, I don't enjoy kissing people, I like the idea of being in a relationship and if it happened I'd be fine with it, but there are definite things that I don't feel comfortable doing. Then about four years ago I thought, "That's who I am. I am an asexual lesbian." It was a bit of a struggle for the first couple of months. I was thinking, "Oh my god, am I going to be alone forever?" but then I realised I'm not really worried about that. Eventually I was pretty chill with it. Then gradually I'd let other people in my life know, if it came up. People know that I'm gay, but because I'm quite private I felt like my sex life or lack thereof is none of people's business anyway.'

Briana and Charlotte's experiences might be relatively common in the grand scheme of things, but aromantic lesbians are a little harder to come by. Apparently, while 1 per cent of the world's population are self-reported asexuals, only 25.9 per cent of those asexuals identify as aromantic. (Data doesn't exist for aromantics who are into sex, perhaps an indication of how much the orientation is misunderstood.) When you consider how many of those aromantics might identify as lesbians, the official numbers get even smaller.

While researching for this book, I spent a lot of time awake at night, scrolling through aromantic forums, Reddit and Quora threads where aromantics share memes and questions and lament about living in a world that prizes romantic love above all other types of love. At first, I honestly didn't get it. I've spent the majority of my life either lusting after someone, being wrapped up in my partner or pining after someone I've lost. Romance is one of my most fundamental and dizzying drives. But after reading through these forums I realised how weird this sounds, as if 'being in love' is my reason for breathing. It's so many others' too: the happy ending of every film, the sparkling climax of our favourite pop songs, the goal we most pursue in life. To aromantics, it must feel as though the rest of the world has been brainwashed. *I don't want a romantic relationship*, writes one user on an aromantic subreddit. *I want to go on a dungeon quest with a Samoyed dog named Tony and a calico cat named Leo to slay a cave beast.*

Others use the forums simply to vent, or express feelings that they feel self-conscious doing so elsewhere: *I have no interest in holding hands, or PDA, or generally doing couple-y things,* writes another. *I've never been in a romantic relationship. The one time I tried, it ended poorly. I do have a long-term FWB, who I care about a lot, but only as a friend. We don't kiss or even touch much unless we're in bed. Even in media, I prefer relationships that feel grounded in connection and mutual understanding, and generally resemble close friendships, rather than traditional romances that to me seem based on some nebulous thing that I can't fully understand.*

When it comes to lesbian aromantic voices online, there's a lot of questioning. *Could I identify as an aromantic lesbian? I have never experienced romantic attraction towards anyone, but I do experience sexual attraction only towards women,* asks one user. *Are there any other aro lesbians out there?* asks another. In a 2014 piece for *VICE*, one twenty-six-year-old aromantic lesbian from the US describes her identity in a way that a lot of lesbians should be able to digest: 'I'd say that the idea of being in a romantic relationship or being in love feels the same way the idea of sleeping with a man does: thoroughly wrong on a visceral level.'

§

Up until my early twenties, I held onto the belief that words meant everything. Every human emotion, every complex in-between state of being, every fleeting thought and in-flux feeling, could be neatly expressed in words, so long as you could summon the right ones. There was no inexpressible, only the as-yet-unexpressed. Language might be in reach or out of reach, but it was always there, winking at you. Speech or writing was the state of grasping it. I devoured books and articles and songs that managed to condense complicated, contradictory feelings into a few heart-wrenching lines. I savoured the satisfaction of pinpointing the perfect sentence, feeling the words click and whirr into action, like the slow, precise mechanism of a wind-up clock. And I'd feel frustrated when that didn't happen, as it often didn't, as if my brain needed oiling and sharpening.

Some philosophers go a step further and believe that language is integral to thought. As in, they're the same thing. Language doesn't just put labels on thoughts, *it is the thoughts*, and without it you'd just have a brain full of formless white noise.

Theorists call this linguistic determinism – or the Sapir–Whorf hypothesis, named after the linguists Edward Sapir and Benjamin Lee Whorf. Although, before them, it was Nietzsche who wrote: 'We cease to think if we do not want to do it under linguistic constraints.' Anyway, this school of thought is largely considered out of fashion and full of holes now (the phrase 'light blue', for instance, doesn't necessarily account for all the different types of light blue that might be dancing around your mind). But for a long time, I clung to this idea that words, if not equal to thoughts, could at least formulate them. It fit neatly into my belief that language was fundamental. This might sound unromantic, but to me it was the opposite: if your words were strange and precise and sparkling, so too could be your understanding of the world, and vice versa.

These days I don't feel so strongly about words, which seems like an unusual thing to write in a book that is full of them. What I mean is: words change and adapt and evolve continuously, and can only go so far in describing reality in all of its shifting parameters and spaces in between. Words cannot account for our subjective, differing realities. Life can also be in feeling, in colour, in the moments between waking up and realising you're awake. In Lynn Steger Strong's 2020 novel *Want*, the main character describes this idea almost exactly: 'All that talking, years of reading: There was a time I thought that all language might contain something of value, but most of life is flat and boring and the things we say are too. Or maybe it's that most of life is so much stranger than language is able to make room for, so we say the same dead things and hope maybe the who and how of what is said can make it into what we mean.'

The language of queerness differs all over the world, meaning common consensuses are impossible to reach in that regard anyway. In Japan, for instance, people rarely use pronouns in direct reference to other people. Words equating to non-binary, agender and genderfluid are also a lot less common in Japan (although towards the latter 1990s, queer organisations popularised the term 'X-gender', similar to non-binary or genderfluid). Did non-binary or genderfluid people exist in Japan before such a word was in use? Of course they did. There just wasn't an adequate term to describe it.

'Lesbian' might have started out as something straightforward: a term to describe those from the island of Lesbos and then later a word to describe women who have sex with other women. But it's gone through endless evolutions in the centuries since, so much so that it's hard to know where one definition begins and the other ends. Lesbian is a word that denotes sex and romance, gender, politics and history, culture and community, but not always at the same time. Lesbian is a word that means a lot of things and nothing definitive at all.

To write about lesbian culture, then, or to write about queerness in general, is to write about something that is ephemeral and sometimes impossible to grasp. It's to write about something that means different things to different people. A lot of those reading this might disagree with this definition of things. If you believe that lesbians are only ever one thing (women who exclusively have sex with women, for instance), then lesbian culture is just the collective manifestation of that one thing through time. But if we are to believe that lesbians can be lots of things, that it's not always to do with sex or gender or intimacy or one specific community, how those things are questionable and mutable anyway, then we can see that lesbianism exists in a continuum. There isn't one way to be a lesbian, just as there isn't one way to be bisexual, to be a woman, or to be in love. When I call myself a lesbian, it's not because I've assembled a list of satisfactory evidence and presented it to a board of older lesbians (although if there is such a thing, I'd like to apply please). It's because

I know it to be true, in my gut. And, like all things, this identity might change. I might be a lesbian today but who knows what I will become years into the future, when I will have hopefully learned more about myself and my surroundings than what I currently hold to be true.

One of my favourite (of many) definitions of lesbian isn't a particularly modern one. It appears in an 1982 essay titled 'New Notes On Lesbianism', written by the Black lesbian feminist poet and scholar Cheryl Clarke. In it, she expresses the full weight of the word 'lesbian' and what it means to her, with crisp, brilliant clarity: 'I name myself "lesbian" because this culture oppresses, silences, and destroys lesbians, even lesbians who don't call themselves "lesbians". I name myself "lesbian" because I want to be visible to other Black lesbians. I name myself "lesbian" because I do not subscribe to predatory/institutional-ized heterosexuality. I name myself lesbian because I want to be with women (and they don't all have to call themselves "lesbi-ans"). I name myself "lesbian" because it is part of my vision.'

CHAPTER TWO

Coming Out

S ome people have always known they're gay. They spend their early years completely disenchanted with the opposite sex and escape at the earliest opportunity to pursue a life of zine launches and John Waters film marathons. Others never really know. They get married to their childhood sweetheart, assume that sex is supposed to be a clinical yearly thing and occasionally wake up in the night sweating and wondering why they dreamt about Rachel Weisz in an eighteenth-century trouser suit for the third time that week.

I don't fit into either category – although obviously there are a million shades of grey in between. I spent most of my childhood and teenage years assuming I was straight, because that's what the outside world generally teaches us we are. But queerness crept up slowly, and then all at once, like clouds gathering before a release. And it's only when I look back – peering closely at each interaction, fleeting intimacy and emotion for 'clues' – that I realise nothing is that simple. Like, maybe I've always been a raging dyke. Or maybe nobody is ever one fixed thing. We just are what we are in the moment, then we try to shape it into some sort of narrative later.

I don't really remember my very first crushes – but there were probably multiple. At primary school I was much more interested in the women teachers than the men. In a pattern that would last long into the future, I was desperate to know the inner workings of their mind, their habits, the things they were proud of, *definitely* the things they weren't. The men were nice enough, they were fine, but to me the women seemed to hold secrets behind curling Marlboro smoke, complicated strengths beneath sweet nineties-brand perfumes and words that were there but unspoken, lingering in the spaces between the blink of an eyelid, or the slow turn of a head.

Back then, these feelings didn't strike me as particularly meaningful or romantic. I was just a kid, probably only about eleven or twelve. But it's only when you look back and survey the tray of evidence that your personal story begins to unfurl itself. One time, in the school corridor, I started shouting to a friend about something – I don't remember what. I think I said I was sick of people mistaking me for a boy because I wore 'boy' jeans and had a weird, homemade haircut that made me look like a very small Richard Ashcroft. One of the teachers walked by, overhearing, and briskly leaned into my ear. 'Don't take stereotypes so seriously,' she whispered, and then she was gone, leaving the smell of instant coffee and fag ash behind her.

The feeling that brief interaction (and a few others like it at the time) gave me – some strangely feminine, ungraspable sense of longing, and knowing – was like a vague seed planted in my gut; a 'clue'. And over the years, those seeds grew, until eventually they flowered.

§

A lot of lesbians describe their formative experiences with boys as feeling distinctly 'wrong'. Their scrabbling hands, their heavy bones. PlayStations and pillows without cases on. Stale smoke and big sports socks and jabbing, *always jabbing*. I didn't feel that way. I enjoyed the company of boys. I liked kissing them. They turned me on. When I was thirteen, I would make my boyfriend lie on his belly so I could tweeze all the hairs out of his back moles. We would lie in the grass for hours until our T-shirts were streaked green and our heads thick and heavy with sunshine. His tongue tasted like chlorine, and I can still picture his body, long and stretched out beneath the white moonlight splashing through his bedroom window.

But as I got older, things got harder. Men wanted different things. They felt sturdier, more threatening somehow, their legs like tree trunks that could pin you down. The idea that I had to 'lose my virginity' to a man – because at that age it was always *had to*, never *wanted to* – felt like a strange yet necessary form of self-inflicted violence, one that needed to happen right away. When it eventually did – at sixteen, to a dubstep-obsessed Turkish boy from Finsbury Park who kept all his Tarantino DVDs on display – it was as if I had already begun to separate men from intimacy. I could have sex with men, that was fine, oftentimes it was fun, but I experienced none of the overwhelming desire I'd seen in films, none of the closeness that had come so easily when I was younger.

Friends would tell me to wait a few years and everything would fall into place. 'Sex is shit when you're a teenager, honestly it's supposed to get better,' they would impart wisely over shared roll-ups, hidden between cars at lunchtime in our customised school uniforms and black Topshop plimsolls. I believed them. I envisioned a future of unbridled shagging with a Robert-Mapplethorpe-look-a-like boyfriend. We'd take turns snapping black-and-white Polaroids of each other naked, blurry, pinning them to our duck-egg coloured Smeg fridge (the surest sign that you've made it) and reenact our favourite film lines out loud. *My time will come*, I told myself, like a mantra. *My time will come.* And it did, of course, just not in the way I thought it might.

My first tangible crush on a woman hit me like a car in the dark. It was not something I'd experienced before, or even knew what to do with. But that's how everything feels when you're sixteen, hormonal, open to anything. Whenever her name pinged up on my BlackBerry screen in electric blue I'd start sweating and breathing dramatically, suddenly the imagined star of my own lesbian TV drama. This is what desire is supposed to feel like, *this is real desire*, I'd think, delirious, shocked at this newfound awareness inside myself. For a brief window of time, there was suddenly nothing more overtly appealing than her blood-coloured hair, her slate grey eyes, her hungover voice that would carry from one side of the street to the other like a reversing lorry. 'Hi babe,' she would whisper down the phone, sadly in that way adults are sad, and I would sway from side to side, trying not to be sick.

She was straight, patently straight (aren't they all?). She was so straight that she didn't care about not being straight sometimes. And when we finally touched each other, drowsily, inconsequentially over one sticky summer, I felt like a sea creature whose shell had finally been cracked open. There was no bristling stubble or forceful, grabbing hands. There was no blankness inside where there should have been feeling. No waking up alone surrounded by darkness and someone else's damp sweat. It was more instinctive than that, much softer. When she kissed me unexpectedly once, I remember feeling like I wanted to climb inside her mouth and inhabit her skin for a while. I would have let her swallow me whole back then. Every movement was a revelation, or at least the promise of something new. My first glimpse into a prism of infinite, possible futures

– none of them the ones I'd been told I should have, but all of them the ones I wanted.

Desire is often what shifts your perspective as a queer person, what pushes you closer to understanding yourself (or coming out). And when I speak to other queer people about this all-important shift in perspective, they often point to a similar event, of feeling something too big inside to keep caged up and tethered. How desire is a force of its own, you can't control it or direct it in ways that you'd prefer. You have to grow and move with your queerness, or else you might end up destroying yourself.

§

Coming out is wildly different for everybody and generally incites various colours of trauma and joy, depending on the situation. I grew up in east London in the mid- to late 2000s, meaning that, unlike a large majority of my queer mates, I never went through the acute isolation of living in a near-empty seaside town or countryside location in which the only gay club is twenty-three miles away and called something like 'LUCYS'. Instead, for me, queerness was always there, but just out of reach. I'd watch lesbians with black fades and matching lipstick fall out of The George and Dragon on Hackney Road while I scuttled out of Tesco Express. I'd pore through flash-on party candids of girls with their tongues in other girls' mouths in *i-D* magazine at the off-licence. I'd peer at genderless couples in leggings and mullets holding hands through the school gates. Something about them rang true and deep. I craved that same authenticity; it was just a case of locating it within myself.

I was also fortunate – or simply privileged – in the sense that my family never assumed things about my sexuality. They didn't push heteronormativity onto me in conscious ways, which helped enormously. My mum never howled at the prospect that she might never have grandchildren (some straight people don't want kids; some queer people do and can). My grandmother, a perennial hippy with an open mind and a sharp tongue, seemed to prefer that I was queer anyway. She'd lend me books like *Lux the Poet* by Martin Millar, or one of the many Sarah Waters stories she had stacked in dusty piles around the house. The rest of my family – mostly women; loud, brilliant, argumentative women – were more interested in the gossip and logistics of a situation, rather than necessarily the genders of those involved.

As such, I didn't feel the need to sit everybody around a dinner table and announce the gender identities of those I'd decided to sleep with, like they do in films, usually followed by the dad staring tight-lipped out a window and the mum quietly sobbing in a floral apron. I didn't create a WhatsApp group called 'I have decided to eat pussy. Thoughts?' and invite everyone I've ever known to join. I didn't write a handwritten letter, explaining how Miss Honey in *Matilda* is *more* than just Miss Honey. Instead, when me and the girl I was seeing at uni started getting more serious, I texted my mum to inform her that we were no longer just friends. I don't remember her response. It might have been 'cool'. And then we all went back to our lives, as if I'd announced that I was considering getting into mosaic collecting, or laser tag.

In later years, therapists would try to mine me for trauma surrounding my coming out. They didn't understand that trauma doesn't always have its route in queerness; you can be healthy in your queerness and fucked-up everywhere else. Or, more accurately, the initial coming out itself isn't always the only and original source of anguish. There's everything that happens afterwards. There's the coming out that you have to do time and time again elsewhere, there's the actual world you end up living in – but how do you put that into words? It would take me years before I realised the effect that coming out – in a more general and repetitive sense – had on my psyche, on how I viewed my place within the rest of society.

For many, of course, that initial coming out is often an immensely traumatic and even dangerous experience. A lot of people never do it. One person I spoke to, Eli, a twenty-seven-year-old non-binary lesbian, told me that their family household was so religious and conservative that coming out was simply not an option. For someone who had known they weren't straight or cis from around age five, this was a dysphoric and oppressive way to live. It ate away at their insides like an invisible parasite, one they longed to rip away. 'My parents had been openly homo-phobic my entire life,' Eli tells me over FaceTime in between shifts from their retail job. 'They are the kind of people who, if you'd do something wrong, they'd tell you how you'd be dead and buried in the backyard before the cops came. So I was not going to come out as gay *and* trans in that house . . . Not in a million years.'

Instead, Eli 'just focused the entirety of high school on getting as many marks as possible, always appearing busy and spending as much time as possible out of my parents' way.' It didn't help that those early years were spent in an intensely claustrophobic farming community with a population of around 400 people. 'Everybody knew me by my parents' names. I was "their daugh-ter", and that's what people would call me,' Eli says, laughing down the phone before becoming quiet. 'My actions were reported on; who I talked to, where I went. It was super religious; a lot of people participated in the Quiverfull movement. There was a purity club. Being honest about my background [back then] was just . . . not possible.'

Eli eventually escaped their hometown to go to uni, found their own queer community of like-minded individuals and decided to sever contact with their parents three years ago. They're still not entirely sure if their parents know they're queer, or if they just choose to ignore it and remain in denial.

Eli's situation might have been particular, specific, but their story is not a rare example of the formative queer experience. Many people I spoke to described the ways in which their sexuality was still a source of contention among their families, sometimes in explicit ways like being called homophobic slurs, or being kicked out of their family home, but very often in more implicit ways, like their partner being referred to as their 'friend' at family events, or not mentioning them to those outside the family circle due to discomfort or shame. Homophobia in any shade can do lasting damage.

There's also the misconception that recognising your own queerness happens right at the age you're beginning to think about sex, or romance, and then it's a straightforward journey after that. But that's simply not true. For some people I spoke to, they didn't fully realise their own queerness until later on in their lives, and it was still something they didn't have a firm grasp on. Sexuality – and gender – can often feel fluid, they're ever-changing, so our ideas of what we're into, or who we *are*, evolve accordingly. For those who identify as bisexual or pansexual, the coming out journey can be a complex and fluctuating balancing act. It doesn't help that you're either 'going through a phase' according to the straight people that surround you, or else 'not queer enough' to be accepted among the queer community.

Ruby, a twenty-five-year-old bisexual woman, tells me that her coming-out story was drawn out and complicated due to a number of external factors, some of which I personally relate to. 'The first time I came out was to myself, and it was a surprise to me,' she remembers. 'It's only been recently, in the past year even, that I've been going back and addressing my past – whether that be my childhood, my early sexual experiences, all the references I have of being a woman – and looking at them again with a queer lens. I guess I'd been taught to put all of those feelings, which were sexual and romantic, into a space of "girl crushes" and admiring women.'

Once she'd come out to herself, tentatively at first, and then enthusiastically later, she didn't feel the need to make some sort of announcement, partly because it wasn't as simple as 'going from straight to gay, or gay to straight. It was a slow burner'. But she eventually had a chat with her mum about it. 'My mum is really supportive and liberal,' she says, 'But I had to have that conversation. There have been lots of lovely sexual women in my life, but I had to explain that even if I'd never slept with a woman, this is still my sexuality, and it is still valid. I think because all the people I'd introduced had been male partners, in her mind it was like, "when Ruby brings a woman home, that's when her sexuality changes", when actually it's not like that.'

Ruby has also had to navigate her feelings toward queer spaces, and her presence within straight-leaning ones too (aka most of them). 'As a femme woman, I am never read – unless I'm making out with a woman in a club – as a queer woman,' she mulls over, when I ask if she's ever faced challenges in either scenario. 'But the queer communities are growing so much in London right now, which is beautiful, so the spaces I fall into are queer in a way that most people there fancy more than one gender. I don't have much experience being in exclusively women-to-women spaces because I still have some insecurity around that I guess, and some hostility towards not feeling "gay enough" or whatever. For me personally, it's easier when I date and sleep with other people who are bi because they get it, and there is still such a stigma.'

Despite the fact lesbians and bisexual women have a lot in common, Ruby's right. The relationship between these communities isn't always seamless. I've known plenty of lesbians who have rolled their eyes upon finding out the girl they fancy is bi, assuming that they'll 'go back to men after experimenting', or else feeling hostile towards the fact they're considered part of the straight community too. The source of these insecurities is clear. Many of us have had experiences with bi or publicly straight-identifying women that have left us feeling like a lesbian holiday – fine for a secret fling, but way too shameful to introduce to the parents like a 'real' partner (According to one 2013 Pew Research LGBT Survey, 84 per cent of bisexual people end up in straight relationships). When biphobia persists in both straight and queer communities though, it's no wonder many opt for the relative simplicity of heteronormative partnerships (and I say 'simplicity' lightly because, as one bi friend wryly pointed out, 'dating straight men is, famously, a carnival of humiliation'.) Equally, bi people shouldn't be forced to justify which genders they are currently romantically involved with, and their choices needn't be constantly theorised about either. In essence, biphobia creates a double bind. And it can leave many of those who identify as bi feeling like a sense of belonging is not possible, their existence eradicated into nothingness, their sexuality dictated to them by other people based on insecurities, misunderstandings and presumptions.

§

Coming out, as a concept, is particularly important when we speak about queer culture. Once you come out – first to yourself, to your friends and possibly family afterwards, to the people you meet along the way, or whatever order your life decides to spread itself out in front of you like unruly, scattered marbles – you're left to discover a shared understanding among those who are similar to you. You might meet other queer people at some point, you might hook up with them, date them, love them, make enemies out of them. You might be drawn to films and TV shows with queer leads and storylines. You might listen to music that speaks to your experiences or absorb art and fashion that more readily reflects your state of mind.

Slowly, eagerly, you might immerse yourself in online spaces that exist separately to the straight world you grew up in, the one that stifles you. You might find solace in queer nightlife and club culture, or you might find it in fiction, in the works of queer authors and poets. Crucially, you might discover, as I did, that the culture of lesbians and bi people has existed for as long as queer women have (aka forever) and therefore so has a shared language, even when that language has been subjugated and pushed into the underground. You might also recognise that LGBTQ people and their culture are not one and the same, and that among many of us there's a tension between the wish to assimilate and a desire to tear down the systems we find oppressive.

My own immersion in queer culture happened gradually – or at least I think it did. Culture is such a nebulous, obscure concept that it's difficult to pinpoint specific moments in time. One second you might be singing 'Mr Brightside' at karaoke with your side-stepping Lego-haired boyfriend, and the next you've hacked off most of your fringe, inserted not one but two rings into your septum and can recite every word from the little-known BBC drama *Lip Service* (both series), with no knowledge of how you got from one to the other.

Having a long-term girlfriend definitely pushed me further into the queer world. She'd been out for years and had a long line of stressful exes and a network of gay girl mates who would reference *The L Word* like a second language.

My best friend Shauna identifies as queer, too. She came out not long after we met. So, when my ex and I broke up at the same time she broke up with hers, we threw ourselves even deeper into lesbian and bi culture in a bid to heal ourselves. We cut each other's hair with blunt scissors to look 'gayer', swapped detailed notes over WhatsApp about which brands sell the best strap-ons (Sh!) and spent countless nights eating vegan cheese on her bedroom floor, cackling through shockingly badly acted lesbian movies like *Below Her Mouth* and *Loving Annabelle*.

Because at its core, culture is a shared thing. It's the manifestation of collective experience. You might get bang into Virginia Woolf and Angela Davis out of your own volition, or spend solitary nights crying to the first MUNA album with the curtains closed, but ultimately, it's only once you have a network of queer people around you – online or IRL – that this sense of community and its culture really flourishes. It's a privilege not everyone's lucky enough to experience, but it's significant, nonetheless. And from my perspective, the process of coming out and those first tentative steps into queer culture have always been intrinsically interlinked.

I spoke to my friend Coco about this. She works as a DJ and producer and spends a lot of time in gay clubs – working or otherwise. But it hasn't always been this way. Now aged twenty-eight, Coco says her late teens and early twenties were spent trying to 'find her people', or just feel less alone. Like many of us, she felt isolated back then, and confused about who she was. 'I started realising maybe when I was, like, fourteen?' she says when we chat about the complex, private process of coming out to ourselves. 'At first it just felt like curiosity. But when I realised it was more sexual . . . I went into deep self-hatred mode. I'd been brought up really homophobic. My family would tut at visibly queer people in the street – all that horrible stuff. So then it was suddenly directed inwards, to myself.'

It's weird to hear Coco speak about a time before she was out and proud. I first met her in early 2017, at Dalston Superstore, a beloved east London queer club and semi-regular haunt of ours. She was playing a bunch of very loud dirty club tunes, had her angular hair dyed powdery silver and was probably wearing a vegan-leather beret. That night, Shauna and I ended up drinking vodka schnapps on her living-room floor while she showed us her assortment of PVC harnesses. Her and Shauna had been on a few Tinder dates, but it hadn't amounted to much. They were better off as friends. So now we could all be friends, together. As far as introductions go, it doesn't get much more lesbian than that.

Rewind ten years, though, and Coco's only reference to lesbian culture was *Sugar Rush* and *The L Word* – two TV shows she absorbed enthusiastically and in secret, just like the majority of closeted girls throughout the 2000s. 'I had a TV with a DigiBox, which meant I could watch *Sugar Rush*, and then I could watch the repeat on Channel 4 +1,' she says. We both cackle. I tell her I relate. 'That was a big deal for me. Then I discovered *The L Word*, which was a major part of me becoming more comfortable with myself. I used to rip old seasons off UTorrent, pretending I was doing homework. Then I'd upload it to my iPod and watch it upstairs, in secret, under the duvet.'

Coco soon discovered Our Chart online – a short-lived social networking site for lesbian and bi women that was based on *The L Word*. Coco says it was integral to her coming-out experience. She met a bunch of queer girls from Bristol on the site and would drive down from her hometown of Rugby to meet one of them, hanging out at gay bars in the city and slowly inching her way out of the closet. It was around this time she started easing into her own identity, making out with girls and getting into gay nightlife. By the time she went to uni, she was ready to be out. And by the time she moved to London – a few years before we met – she was fully primed to throw herself face-first into queer culture.

'I moved to a youth hostel on Shoreditch High Street and that's when the "gay stuff" really happened,' she tells me, laughing when I press her to pinpoint the moment she went from baby dyke to seasoned queer. 'I was quite comfortable with my sexuality at this point, but I just didn't know where to go. So me and my friend Adam discovered The Joiners Arms . . . Do you remember those rubber meat flaps? And the sticky pool table, the smoking area, the toilets guys were definitely banging in . . . that place was fucking genius. And then it was Dalston Superstore. And then I think just through dating people . . . it just went from there.'

What gradually becomes clear when speaking to Coco and other queer people, and from my own late-night conversations with myself, is that coming out has never been one singular, corporeal thing. It's not like you're raised straight, and then you rip off the coming-out plaster and carry on with life as before, except a gayer version of it. Rather, it differs for everybody, and it's a never-ending process. Your sexuality doesn't always remain fixed either – it fluctuates over time, like a best friend from childhood who you thought you knew like a birthmark, but who actually holds secrets, things they aren't telling you, things they possibly never will.

I don't think these processes are solely confined to the identities of queer people, either. We all contain multitudes and parts of ourselves that we don't recognise yet, parts of ourselves that differ from the structures we have been raised with. We all look at ourselves in the mirror sometimes and think, 'Who *are* you, though? What have you *come* here for? What do you *want* for yourself?' These inward-facing questions are as old as time itself. They are an integral part of the human condition. The only difference is, queer people are forced to take these private reflections and hold them up to the light, for everybody else to see and evaluate. It's a strange position to find yourself in, for sure, but I also think it can be intrinsically beneficial. Everyone could learn something from queer people. Because what could be more valuable than assuming nothing about ourselves or others, and then slowly, over time, learning everything?

And if you asked me where that journey so often begins, I'd answer without missing a beat: the club.

CHAPTER THREE

The Club

It is 2008 and you are wasted. Really wasted. The only reason you know this is because you are walking through the streets of Hackney at 12 a.m. and you are singing the Charles & Eddie song 'Would I Lie to You?', which you usually hate. Every note comes out like a warbling screech. You continue, trying to make each line more controlled than the next, but instead it gets worse, your voice getting louder, battering the outside walls of the houses nearby. The houses with their curtains closed and their lights off and their black shadow lawns. The families in these houses have gone to sleep. But you are only just waking up.

You are sixteen. You are sixteen and wearing a bodycon dress from American Apparel, which is a shop that hasn't yet gone into liquidation or been rocked by a series of sexual assault scandals. You are sixteen and your fringe is straightened and plastered to one side, which is the way fringes have been worn for most of the decade, although that is just about to change. You are sixteen and you are not alone: you are with three people in their twenties who are taking you to a gay bar for the very first time. In future years, one of these people will become a doctor on the frontline of the COVID crisis. Another will get married, twice, and move to Spain. You've never been sure what happened to the third. But in that moment, you are all walking together and you are singing and you cannot feel the midnight blue cold because you are sixteen and you *literally* do not care (that is how you pronounce the word 'literally' – as if it is always in italics).

The gay bar you are walking to is called The Joiners Arms and it has been around for twenty years, which is longer than you have been alive. Twenty years of sweat and twenty years of spilled spirits all over the floor and twenty years of saliva and sex and smoking inside, although by the time you arrive the smoking ban has just come into effect and now you can only smoke outside, in a small concrete yard, surrounded by stonewashed denim, swinging crucifix earrings, topless boys in tracksuit bottoms, crushed chips and dimpled skin. Inside, there is a tattered pool table that gets pushed to one side when people want to dance and there's a rotten old fruit machine in one corner and a bedraggled-looking drag queen who is there every night, 'entertaining'. She smells vividly and stubbornly like body odour, but you don't care; no one cares.

At night they play UK garage and *Scary Monsters*-era Bowie and The Gossip and regular glossy chart-pop like The Pussycat Dolls, in no particular order – although Sundays are dedicated to techno, and Tuesdays to karaoke. They are always open until 4 a.m., apart from Mondays, and they do not check your ID or care when you go to the toilet with a hairy-chested bear called Big Jim and an old lesbian with a shaved head called Sue and come out excited and wired and, wow, you cannot believe that such a place exists. You cannot believe that life can feel like this. *I am going to do this for so long*, you think to yourself, now just a sticky body and two black pupils beneath pink and purple dappled lights. *I am going to do this for so long, until I am old and shrivelled and physically eroded from all these years of freedom*. You are in some ways wrong about that – life would become unrecognisable, as it tends to, like a creature you accidentally gave birth to – but you wouldn't have believed me back then, even if I'd told you.

You do not yet know that you are queer, but you do not know that you aren't queer either, and you don't think about it too deeply because you are just here to dance. All you know is that The Joiners Arms makes you feel happy and at peace with yourself and others. Something about the actual building – the tobacco-coloured frontage, the tail-end of Hackney Road, the desolate car wash opposite – makes you want to come back, all the time. In later years, when your sexuality becomes more central to your modes of interaction and way of being, The Joiners Arms is still one of the only nightlife spots in which you feel properly free and comfortable in your own skin. It makes you swell and click into place. Admitting that out loud feels overly earnest and slightly po-faced, but if you were to speak honestly to yourself in private, at your own reflection, that is probably what you would say because that is the truth.

Months and then years will pass after that first night at the gay club. During the expanse of time after 2015 – when The Joiners Arms is boarded up and abandoned and covered in a thin, then thick layer of dust – people will try to describe the energy of the place in online 'looking back' essays and nostalgic pub conversations. There will be a tireless campaign to try to save it, which sort of works but mainly doesn't because it never actually comes back. It's supposed to be turned into offices, or exactly nine luxury flats – you can't quite remember – but instead it just sits there, empty, for years into the future. You too will try to bottle its spirit and explain it in a book. But the words won't sound right. You'll start to forget what it felt like in there sometimes. The memories in your mind will resemble images of a documentary about a different time experienced by somebody else, as if they are two, maybe three degrees of separation from yourself.

Did The Joiners even exist in the way we thought it did, you'll wonder in those moments. Because The Joiners could be shitty too, you're sure of it. What about the stench of the place, those times it took a rough turn. The crowds of men that sometimes took over, eyes glinting in shadowy corners. One night, you'll remember darkly, your girlfriend at the time was spiked. You carried her into a taxi, then tried to drag her upstairs, hands under armpits, but it was a struggle. The medical worker at the end of the phone told you to make sure she was lying on her side and that it would probably wear off in the morning. You lightly slapped her face a few times. She burbled and drooled. Her eyes rolled back into her head. The next morning she couldn't remember a thing past putting a drink to her lips. She laughed about it, burying the anxiety, the way we're taught to. Yeah, The Joiners could be shitty too. Not every queer space is a safe space. You think about that too sometimes.

But other times, briefly, when you are walking down a polluted street at night-time in winter, or spot a flash of baby-blue neon lighting, or smell a trace of stale cloying sweat and dried up Marlboro Reds, you'll remember the joy that used to live there. Or your body will at least. And your chest will ache for a moment. Something here has been lost, it will tell you. Because bodies hold onto things like this. Bodies don't forget the things that they are missing.

§

These days, when we think of east London, we think of tech start-ups and branches of Pret a Manger stacked with identical triangular sandwiches to be consumed quickly on lunch breaks. We think of white city boys in brown shoes and jeans finishing work at 5.30 p.m. and getting a few pints in at the Big Chill. We think of hotels and high rises, bank chains and Byron Burgers, late-night Subway joints nestled up against gastro pubs that used to be old man pubs that will soon become nothing. We think of construction sites – bulldozers, diggers and posters advertising luxury flats – and we think of vegan doughnut shops and cafés with millennial pink lights and millennial pink walls that will end up as millennial pink pictures on glistening white screens.

Parts of east London look the same as they did ten, twenty, thirty years ago. Parts of east London even look as if they could have been transported straight out of a Victorian novel. 'Two plants for a *fiiiiivah*!' they shout down Columbia Road every Sunday, as they always have done and always will do until we can no longer grow or sell plants. Brick Lane smells like salt-beef bagels and London Fields remains bustling and green in spring, damp brown in winter, burnt yellow in summer. But the area has also been changing forever, long before any of its current residents arrived. This is a place whose essence is constantly rearranging itself, like a coral reef at the bottom of the sea. And as with inner city neighbourhoods across the globe, evolution is part of its character.

Rewind to the late 1990s and 2000s, and east London was considered by many to be a sort of queer mecca. A combo of art school kids, fashion students and LGBTQ clubbers lived and worked there, which is often the case during the early stages of gentrification: right before property developers get their claws into a low-rent, high-culture area. (See: Berlin, Paris, New York, certain parts of Los Angeles. Some sociologists, like Sharon Zukin, have even theorised that LGBTQ residents actually boost property prices because we cultivate and gravitate towards creativity. The lesbians get priced out of other areas and settle into new ones, the gay men follow their lead, the gay men then build the institutions because they earn the money, and eventually the straight people arrive. The lesbians get pushed out and the process starts all over again. It's just a theory – and it's also intimately bound up with class and race, not just queerness – but there's a glimmer of truth in there somewhere.)

East London's reputation for being a queer neighbourhood back then came down to a multitude of factors – the people who rented there, obviously, the places they hung out. But a lot of it was down to the clubs, which were having a moment. They were cooler, younger and grottier than the clubs in Soho, which were slowly becoming shiny, cocktail-slick establishments. They were less cruisy or testosterone-fuelled than those in Vauxhall. Spaces like The Joiners Arms, The George and Dragon, Nelson's Head and, later, clubs like East Bloc, fostered a sense of community; made going out in east London feel exciting, like the night was a big expanse that belonged to you rather than the other way around. The 'straighter' clubs played the wrong music. They were full of cheek-boned indie lads in leather jackets and pretty girls with fringes, no dancing. But the East End gay clubs and nights were alive and colourful and filthy, crammed with zigzag leggings, zebra-print creepers, Peaches on the speakers, dykes everywhere.

I am not old enough to remember the majority of this golden era. In the early- to mid-2000s, I was more likely to be found revising for my mock GCSEs while listening to 'Glamorous' by Fergie on my Motorola flip phone. But the tail-end of that decade, as a teenager, was spent discovering what it meant to Go Out properly. And if I close my eyes, I can just about recall what it felt like around east London during that time: the feverish lightness after hours, the yellow-red flashes of night buses, the bitter taste of MDMA stirred into lukewarm Tyskies to be consumed on the street in between roll-ups. There were options back then, too, and they felt endless: Would we go there or there? Should we get a bus or walk? Which clubs are open all night, and whose flat might we end up at later? How many people might be able to afford an Addison Lee?

These options soon dried up, quicker than we realised they had even been a choice. By the time the 2000s made way for the 2010s, many of the city's most beloved LGBTQ clubs were closing down, one by one, until they were eventually non-existent (none of the clubs I've mentioned so far are still around). This was the case across the capital. One report, published by University College London Urban Laboratory, revealed that London had around 127 venues in 2006. By 2017, that number had dwindled to just fifty-three, meaning we'd lost more than half of our LGBTQ venues in the space of a decade – usually to make way for unaffordable housing, another grey stack of offices, a new fluoro-lit branch of Tesco Express.

This wasn't just a London thing either. In urban areas across the UK, the picture unfolded in very similar ways. Manchester's Canal Street – a gay village once crammed with neon-lit clubs, darkrooms, fetish spaces – gradually evolved into a hotspot for wasted students and straight people on hen dos. Rising house prices in Brighton meant that LGBTQ homeowners would flee to London to work and party, leading to an identity crisis in the area. Glasgow, Birmingham, Bristol, Nottingham, Liverpool – there was not one city in the UK left unaffected by the wave of gay club closures throughout the mid-2000s to 2010s. In 2015, the Association of Licensed Multiple Retailers reported that in 2005 there were 3,144 clubs across the UK. In the space of a decade, that number had become 1,733.

Eventually there would be new nights, new clubs, new faces, different versions of community, different ways in which people would gather (more on that later). But gay nightlife as we'd known it was dying. And by the time the curtains had closed on the 2010s, it was basically already dead.

§

If there's one person who remembers the evolution of these decades clearly, it's Bishi Bhattacharya. She grew up in Earl's Court – an odd part of London that sits right between west and central – with two Bengali parents and an older sister. This was back in the 1990s, at the height of Spice Girls mania, but at twelve years old she was much more into BritPop, like Pulp and Elastica. She'd collect magazines like *The Face* and *Select* to read what they'd been up to. But she also read about the gay clubs, marvelling at the fact they were only twenty minutes down the road from her house. *This is where I should be*, she'd think to herself, eyeing up the bold flash photography pressed onto inky paper. The girls' school she went to was full of posh kids who were up themselves, and the Indian community could be snobby in its own way too. *I need to find my people.*

She put an advertisement together for a pen friend, of sorts. Someone who was into the same shit she was into and might be up for swapping records. Then she sent it in to *Select* magazine. Not long afterwards she received a reply, from a strange, pale wiry boy called Patrick Denis Apps – or as he would later be known, Patrick Wolf. A musician. They built up a correspondence. Back and forth, back and forth, all the time. He was the same age as her and very quickly they became best friends. By the time they were both thirteen, they were sneaking into queer and fetish clubs around Soho. And by the time they were fourteen, they had already begun to make names for themselves in the area, helped in part by the fact they'd started hanging around with Minty, a club kid band/performance artist collective founded by the late Leigh Bowery in the 1980s. During the day, Bishi was getting good grades at her posh school and remaining the picture-perfect South Asian daughter. But by night, it was Bishi whose image was now in the inky club sections of the magazines she had pored over just two years prior.

When I told some of my friends that I was working on this chapter and wanted to get a proper feel for how queer club culture had evolved over the years, particularly around this area, particularly outside of cis gay male spaces, many of the older ones pointed me straight to Bishi. She had been a 'face', they said, around Soho. She was there for the rise and fall of queer Shoreditch. And she was still around today: producing, making music, DJing, running nights and appearing on line-ups in clubs. 'Some people go to university, I went to clubs,' she told Alex Gerry, the nightclub photojournalist, in 2019. 'To me that's the best education there is. I gathered people-skills in a nightclub. You can see them at their best and at their worst, at their lightest and at their darkest.'

Bishi is thirty-six now, with huge brown eyes and a syrupy lilting voice, the kind that has the ability to turn any story into a pleasing shape. She wears a dramatic wide-brimmed hat, a black cape-like coat and never walks into a room without being drenched in Stella McCartney perfume. We meet at Dalston Superstore, which miraculously opened in 2009 at a time when the other clubs were shutting down and has managed to thrive ever since. For a moment I worry that it's too dark and sticky in here, that the toilet door clangs too loudly, that I should have arranged to meet somewhere else. But then I remember what we've come to speak about, and the world she has inhabited, and has been inhabiting ever since she put that ad in *Select*.

At some point in the early 2000s, Bishi moved into a place on the corner of Kingsland Road and Old Street with an industrial German musician called No Bra. They paid £400 per month. This was when Soho was becoming almost passé. Queer nightlife had begun to bleed into east London, because 'that was where all the cheap space was'. This coincided with the rise of electroclash, a playful genre imported from Munich that naturally appealed to queer audiences. There were queer nights, but some of them were just electroclash/indie/dance nights, and they each attracted a similar crowd – oftentimes just blending into eachother. 'There was Trash on a Monday, Cheapskates on a Tuesday, Nag Nag Nag at The Ghetto on a Wednesday, Kash Point was the club night I then started running on a Thursday, then there was The Cock at The Ghetto on a Friday,' Bishi says, counting on her fingers. 'The straight stuff tended to happen on a Saturday, I guess. Then on Sunday it was gay stuff, which is when we'd go to The George and Dragon.'

When it comes to where predominantly queer women were hanging out, everyone I speak to is strangely vague (not unusual when it comes to any disscussion about gay nightlife, in which marginalised genders are often considered an add-on within cis male spaces). Some tell me about Club Motherfucker at The Garage, a queer indie night that ran from 2003 to 2013 and naturally attracted a lesbian and bi crowd. Others point to Unskinny Bop, a queer night for girls that used to mainly run at The Pleasure Unit (now The Star of Bethnal Green) down Bethnal Green Road. Generally, though, I get told regularly and often that it was a mixed crowd. Some queer nights might bring in more men, others more women, but it was often more down to the music they were playing than anything more concrete. Maybe they'd play Le Tigre, Chicks on Speed and The Gossip, or maybe they'd play LCD Soundsystem and Erol Alkan. It was that which defined who would end up where, and why.

'I remember there was Candy Bar,' Bishi says, referring to one of the only lesbian and bi clubs that existed back then, alongside a couple of other central spots like She Soho (still open today) and Blush Bar in Stoke Newington (now a PC junk shop according to Google Maps). 'Certain designated spaces for queer women back then tended to be more hardcore lesbian, and those spaces never liked the ones that were a bit more femme. I remember going into Candy Bar when I was fifteen and just getting laughed out of there in my vintage clothes.' But if you wanted to hook up with girls, it wasn't as if those spaces were your only option: far from it. 'When I lived with No Bra, she was out on the prowl all the time,' Bishi adds, laughing. 'At clubs like The Ghetto, everyone just seemed to be getting off with each other.'

Hannah Holland, a lesbian DJ who played a pivotal role in London's alternative and queer club scene throughout the 2000s, remembers this time similarly to Bishi. 'I found it a lot more mixed in terms of gender back then,' she tells me down the phone. 'Trailer Trash, The George and Dragon . . . There was one night – Club Motherfucker – which was brilliant. They had the first gigs of The Gossip and Peaches, and many of those queer female bands and artists who came through would play at Club Motherfucker first. They would play electroclash and punk and riot grrrl, and that was probably a bit more queer-women-led, but it was super mixed and I used to love that.'

Hannah thinks queer club nights became more intentionally segregated later on, after the rise of social media and the way it propagated instant club photography and consequently shaped a night. Obviously lesbian and bi clubs and nights in London existed before then, long before. The first recognised lesbian and bi bar in the capital, the Gateways club, opened as far back as the 1930s and stayed open until the 1980s. But there was a significant moment, says Hannah, when social media pushed club nights to become a little more targeted and specific. Because suddenly events were being advertised on Facebook rather than on flyers or in the back of music mags that only certain people bought. There was more room to see the exact type of crowd they might attract, to tell whether it was for gay and bi men or women.

'In a way, social media pigeon-holed things a little bit,' explains Hannah. 'It categorised nights in a very ordered way. 2006 and 2007 is when Facebook kicked off, and you'd have full-on club photography which would really brand a night, and that's when I noticed more of a separation between men and women when it came to nights.'

Darina, a queer woman in her mid-thirties, moved to London from Ireland around this time, when club nights for lesbian and bi women were becoming more commonplace. She recalls a monthly night called Club Wish that ran at Gramophone in Shoreditch in the mid- to late 2000s. 'Upstairs you'd have pop music and downstairs was house music, but it was all very women-focused,' she says. 'This was before dating apps were a thing. So Wish became so important – to me and my friends anyway. You'd see the same people there every month. You'd start chatting to someone and you'd know you'd see them next time, so you could build up to asking for their number. Wish really hit a moment when it was needed, when you couldn't slide into DMs or match with someone on Hinge.'

In retrospect, this moment was brief. Just when social media had begun to shape how nights were marketed – becoming more specific, catering to different scenes, genders and crowds – the wave of club closures brought many of these nights to a halt before they'd properly hit their stride. It was a complicated time, full of unexpected movement, evolution and loss. Bishi explains it succinctly: 'I would say that there were two things that fundamentally changed going out as I know it. There was the financial crash in 2008, whereby London became a giant members club. And then there was the explosion of social media through smartphone technology.'

Darina stopped going out so much. Hannah got bored and moved to Berlin. By 2009, in her mind at least, the East End queer scene was done for. 'Things started closing down. A scene lights up and has a certain amount of years before we need something new. And I think that coincided with east London, and Shoreditch in particular, becoming oversaturated.'

What does she mean by oversaturated? 'I guess it just wasn't . . . it wasn't really a place for LGBTQ communities anymore.'

§

It is 2018 and you are wasted. Really wasted. The only reason you know this is because you are riding a child's abandoned scooter through the streets of Hackney at 12 a.m., which is the lizard-brain action of somebody you'd usually roll your eyes at. You don't see the jagged piece of pavement that sends your body flying, head hitting a nearby kerb with a neat and comfortable crack. If you had been someone else watching this scene from afar, you would have rolled your eyes a second time.

'I'm fine, I'm fine,' you assure your best friend, who is hovering above you now like a floating head. Her face resembles a jumble of peach-dyed hair and worried expressions. She needs you to get up, you realise, reading her eyes instinctively, so you can both go to the club. There are lesbians in there. There are lesbians and they are waiting. You brush yourself off, fling the scooter in the bush. And then you walk to Dalston Superstore, which is fifteen minutes but also ten years away from where The Joiners Arms used to be. *Nothing much has changed*, you think to yourself distantly, lighting a roll-up and blowing blue smoke into the cold, head still throbbing. *All this time and nothing has changed.*

But everything has changed. iPhones dot the night like stars. When you fall over on the scooter, a friend captures it on video and sends it to you via WhatsApp. You put it on your Instagram story. A few people reply with cry-laughing emojis, someone sends flames. There are more queer women in the DMs than in the club. Those who are in the club have swiped left or right on each other's faces, or they know each other from online. You scroll through Twitter on the loo, scan your Instagram story viewers, reply to a message. You are here, but you are not here. And those who are not here, are here too.

When you leave the club you get into an Uber, which takes you to your door. It knows where your door is because you pre-entered your postcode into an efficient online system that then pre-planned the route via satellite. There is no waiting for a night bus, no stumbling to a different club or seeing where the night may take you. There aren't many more clubs anyway – certainly not queer ones, and none on Sundays. You go to one event and then you stay there. That's how it goes. Even Efes, the all-night Turkish pool club, is shut down now. You know this because you rang their doorbell at 3 a.m. recently to ask. 'We're not open anymore.' A tired voice actually picked up, crackling through the speakers. 'We won't be opening again.'

It is not just club culture that has changed beyond recognition over the past decade, but queer culture too. Conversations are happening. Long overdue ones. They are fizzing under the surface, bubbling up online and on phones and in minds collectively. Conversations about gender. Conversations about sexuality. Conversations about fluidity, the grey matter in between. Conversations about the ways in which binaries have restricted us. Conversations about the binaries within binaries, how they have restricted us too.

These conversations have changed the way people think about nightlife and about space. About who needs what, and why. Ideas about 'queerness' and 'womanhood' have shifted in ways that more accurately reflect the world around us. And, therefore, so have ideas of what a queer space for women looks like, and what it ought to be, and what the purpose of going clubbing is anyway.

§

In 2016, I wrote a piece for *VICE* about how nightlife for queer women in the capital was basically dead. The gay clubs that dominated a decade prior had been closed for years, and it felt like no one was bothering to start nights that catered to a lesbian and bi crowd anymore. Besides, maybe it wasn't such a huge loss. Maybe women simply didn't need queer spaces in the ways we used to. Maybe it wasn't necessarily symptomatic of gentrification and the rise of social media as a replacement for IRL communities, but in fact a sign that society was moving on, that queerness was becoming more mainstream, that 'straight' clubs weren't so much 'straight' clubs anymore, but everything clubs.

This isn't a new conversation. The idea that clubs for queer women (and other genders) are no longer needed has been echoed among a lot of people, in a lot of cities, over the past couple of decades. In a Broadly documentary titled *The Last Lesbian Bars*, queer theorist Jack Halberstam says that 'we weren't accepted anywhere else, so we were forced into creating a subculture where we could feel and find acceptance. But now that we're becoming more integrated into society, you can just walk into a bar down the street and there will be lesbians there holding hands, kissing; there's not that need to find that one spot where you can be yourself.'

In Amin Ghaziani's 2014 book *There Goes the Gayborhood?*, he refers to this era, or this phenomenon even – because if history has taught us anything, it's that attitudes move throughout the world in waves – as 'post-gay'. 'Sexuality has always been an important part of life,' he writes, 'but the recent post-gay shift has been nothing short of startling. Those who consider themselves post-gay profess that their sexuality does not form the core of how they define themselves, and they prefer to hang out with their straight friends as much as with those who are gay. Actually, they do not even distinguish their friends by their sexual orientation.

'This is not to say that people no longer claim a gay, lesbian or bisexual identity for themselves – they do, because sexual orientation is still a part of who we are after all, because heterosexuality is still culturally compulsory, and because sexual inequalities persist,' he continues. 'But with public acceptance of homosexuality and same-sex relationships at an all-time high, it is much easier for some sexual minorities to move into the mainstream, to participate in its most foundational institutions, like marriage or the military, and to blend into the prized, multicultural mosaic in a way that renders them no different from heterosexuals.'

He says 'some sexual minorities' because these ideas are multifaceted, especially when it comes to queer spaces. Making any sort of sweeping statement about their necessity, or lack of, disregards the nuance that exists within 'queerness'. Queer women of colour, for instance, will recognise their needs as different to those of white queer women. Working-class queers will recognise their needs as different to those from wealthier or middle-class backgrounds. Trans people, those who are differently abled, those who live in more rural areas – none of their needs are identical. All these particularities, while sometimes overlapping, make up a wider narrative that is impossible to shove under one umbrella, or even talk about straightforwardly. Which is why the question isn't necessarily about *to what degree* do we need queer spaces, but rather, *what sort* of queer nightlife do certain communities *still need*?

Queer spaces will remain important for as long as queer people are marginalised, and for as long as danger in the public domain persists. Which it does. In a 2017 YouGov polling of more than 5,000 LGBTQ people in Britain, Stonewall reported that 21 per cent of LGBTQ people had experienced a hate crime or incident due to their sexual orientation and/or gender identity within the last twelve months. 29 per cent said that they avoid certain streets because they do not feel safe there as an LGBTQ person, with 44 per cent of them being trans people. And 33 per cent said that they avoid certain bars and restaurants due to fear of discrimination, with 51 per cent of them being trans, and 44 per cent of them being Black, Asian and minority ethnic people.

Public space has not got safer for queer people as time has moved forward. Time cannot be confused with progression. In that same YouGov poll, Stonewall reported that the number of lesbian, gay and bisexual people who had experienced a hate crime or incident in the last year because of their sexual orientation had risen by 78 per cent from 2013 to 2017. In 2019, figures from the Home Office revealed that anti-LGBTQ hate crimes had risen even further, with a 37 per cent increase in transphobic hate crimes, and a 25 per cent increase in homophobic and biphobic hate crimes. In other words, when we speak about assimilation, and question whether certain spaces are still needed for certain communities, we are speaking about a scenario that is fragile and ever-changing, and which differs from person to person, and sometimes year to year.

After writing that piece for *VICE* in 2016, something strange and unexpected happened. Lesbian and bi nights began popping up – here and there at first, and then quite regularly. Not just a couple of random nights on a Tuesday in basements when no one else was around, either. But nights on weekends, in huge, well-attended venues, across the city. Aphrodyki at the Ace Hotel in Shoreditch. Butch, Please! at The Royal Vauxhall Tavern. Nite Dykez, Femme Fraiche and Female Trouble at Dalston Superstore. Gal Pals, Pxssy Palace, LICK events and Big Dyke Energy and many more at various establishments. Just when it had felt as if anyone other than cis gay men had been erased from the club-culture lexicon and were maybe never truly felt there in the first place, a renaissance appeared to be in our midst. But why?

This wasn't the same as the golden era of the East End a decade or so ago, or Soho before then. This was something different, something less static, something more intentional in a heavily gentrified London. And it's difficult to pinpoint exactly what happened, or why this turnaround occurred, but for many, it seems, the creation and sustainment of these nights simply came down to a new sort of perseverance, a blind hope in the face of what felt like the impossible. Later, of course, the COVID-19 pandemic would change everything, bringing every club night – queer, straight, fetish, women, men – to a screeching halt. But in the latter half of 2010s, there was a moment in which lesbian and bi nights reinvented themselves, carving a solid niche within the chequered landscape of UK LBGTQ club culture.

§

I'm sat with a butch lesbian called Tabs in a Scottish-themed café in Leyton, east London, awkwardly alternating sips between an iced coffee and a kale and blue cheese soup (a combination I live to regret). Tabs is drinking tea. She is telling me about her night Butch, Please!, which she started in 2016 and has been running ever since. It's a trans-inclusive night for butch dykes and their friends at The Royal Vauxhall Tavern and, according to Tabs, is the only night of its kind in Europe right now.

'I started it because there was nothing going on. I thought, "I'll just do it then." I didn't have bigger ambitions than that,' she says, pouring more tea into her mug from the pot. 'Although I knew I wanted a space where there were more women. Not "women only" in the traditional sense – obviously inclusive of trans and non-binary people. Just not so many cis men, basically. And I wanted something around me that celebrates butchness. Because I always felt, like, as a butch dyke, just really uncool.'

Tabs is thirty-four now and has lived in London for more than a decade. A lot of that time was spent in LGBTQ clubs. But while these formative nightlife experiences were crucial to her becoming more comfortable in her identity, she often felt that there was a real lack of space for a more butch lesbian crowd. It was almost as if they were at the bottom of the queer totem pole, as if nightlife was perpetually geared towards cis gay men or else femme queer women at a push. 'I definitely felt like I was looked down upon,' Tabs says. 'There just wasn't really a place for that butch stuff in the east London hipster scene.'

And so she filled that gap, with a night 'that celebrates butchness without question, without prejudice'. And Butch, Please! swiftly picked up traction. More recently – or at least before the COVID crisis – it was pulling in around 500 people per night, which is full capacity. 'There was definitely a craving for it. Whatever I felt, other people were feeling as well,' says Tabs. 'Obviously, I wasn't the first. But during this period I believe that Butch, Please! was key in opening up that space again, and holding it open. Because it takes one person to persevere and go, "No, we're going to hold our night in your gay man's bar". It's incredibly hard to hold a space in the world that doesn't make space for us. There are so many more nights going on, but for me, Butch, Please! is the OG.'

Getting the night off the ground wasn't easy. Some in the queer community felt uncomfortable about Tabs' use of the word lesbian during promotion. They viewed it as exclusionary, or in some way reinforcing the gender binary. 'I went to delete the word from the description, but then I stopped and thought, "If I delete this I'm just deleting the fact that I exist, and I do exist",' Tabs says. 'All LGBTQIA people are welcome. I mean, yeah, we don't let groups of cis men in. But other than that, it's a friendly and welcoming night. I'm just saying that if you come, you need to be able to celebrate, understand and respect what butch dyke culture is about. That's all. No big deal.'

Once audiences realised that Butch, Please! wasn't intended or panning out to be an exclusionary space, the criticism died down. Trans masc people party alongside butch lesbians in celebration of their butchness. 'There's this idea that lesbians, butch dykes and trans people are in some sort of battle with each other,' says Tabs. 'I'm not saying those TERFs [trans-exclusionary radical feminists] don't exist and that what they're doing isn't terrible – of course it is. And there are transphobic people and some of them are lesbians and I get that. But that's not all there is. There are loads of trans people at Butch, Please! We party together. And that's existed for a really long time.'

Butch, Please! holds a bi-monthly spot at The Royal Vauxhall Tavern. But for these newer nights, permanent space is a luxury. With a distinct lack of LGBTQ venues across the UK, they usually have to be held in straight clubs and bars, with many changing venues on a regular basis. This comes with its own set of problems: new security and venue staff need to be constantly educated to ensure the space remains safe and LGBTQ friendly.

Plus, it can be harder to foster a regular queer scene or crowd when a club night rarely settles in one location, meaning there's less opportunity for physical communities to flourish. Still, drawbacks like these don't mean that multi-venue nights can't be successful.

Gal Pals has been taking place in London and Brighton in various venues since 2015, although it's become a more regular semi-monthly event since around 2018 (during 2020, when the pandemic kicked off, they switched to virtual parties, which experienced their own surge of popularity). The few times I've been to Gal Pals have been a lot of fun. Crowds of young, excited queer women and non-binary people eyeing each other up. Janelle Monáe, Grimes and Robyn on the speakers. Cheap entry fee. Gal Pals is where you go if you love pop music and want to dance among people like you, maybe hook up with someone who looks like La Roux and tastes like cheap tequila. It's neither overly pretentious in that way east London nights can be, nor devoid of any sense of cool like a uni pride freshers' week mixer. It sits somewhere in between, is its own thing.

Scarlett and Xandice, the couple who run the night, tell me that there has been a 'massive shift' when it comes to queer nights in recent years. It's no longer enough to say 'this is a queer night' like in the 1990s and 2000s or play certain music to bring in a certain crowd. Queer people want spaces that cater to their specific needs, intentionally and intersectionally. 'There's a bigger expectation from our communities to create spaces that are safer, that do uphold certain values and that are able to offer something different than club experiences in the past,' Xandice explains. 'You can say "these spaces are for queer women" or "these spaces are for queer Black people".'

Xandice, who is Black and non-binary, says that creating safe, inclusionary spaces for minorities is really important, but that doesn't mean it's difficult. 'Our ethos from the beginning was that we wanted to have fun and let loose and there doesn't have to be loads of politics on top of that. But we wanted to be clear about who the space is for,' they say.

Scarlett continues: 'It's a night for queer women, trans and non-binary people, but anyone can come – we don't police every single person who comes through the door because that's—' Xandice jumps in: '. . . too prescriptive. And we trust our audience. We have systems in place so we can identify certain situations in the club. People are really aware of how the presence of a large group of men can shift the energy of a space, so it's about making sure it's clear from the get-go that those groups are accompanied.'

'People are expecting that you do more than just put a night on and have cheap drinks,' they add. 'Because we no longer have so much permanent space, the pop-up space has an onus on them to create something that taps into the community a bit more.'

Flo Perry and Hannah Eachus, who have been running their multi-venue night Aphrodyke for the same amount of time in London, say a similar thing: 'The standard for gay male nights compared to lesbian nights is really different. Gay male nights can be like a load of sweaty white guys in harnesses, who are all sample size, in a warehouse, and everyone's like "Wow"; and the logo is literally a penis and it's called something like "Pump". But with lesbian and bi nights, you have to explicitly say that you're not a TERF and show how many steps you're taking to ensure this. Which is good, obviously. It's good we do that. But the standard is different.'

Despite these expectations, Flo and Hannah also agree that it's not difficult to adhere to them. 'The hardest thing about being an inclusive lesbian night is that venues will still try and put you in the basement,' says Flo, laughing. 'Other than that, it's easy . . . We are inclusive. We just have to say we are, constantly.'

When I speak to the people behind Butch, Please!, Gal Pals and Aphrodyki about the future of their nights, and of clubbing for lesbian and bi people in general, they each mention the fact that there needs to be more outside of London, that they'd like to take their nights elsewhere, that people in Bristol, Liverpool, Manchester, Birmingham would benefit from having more places to go.

Ultimately, Hannah tells me, 'It's not that difficult to run a club night, and more people should.'

Flo agrees: 'Every time I get a complaint from someone at Aphrodyki being like, "Why don't you get a bigger venue, why don't you do it more often?" I'm like . . . start your own fucking club night so *I can go to it*. We started Aphrodyki because it was our ideal club night. But I just want someone to start one on a Saturday that's five pounds and I will be there. And I can relax. And if a lightbulb falls off the ceiling then I won't have to worry about it.'

When I speak to people about growing up queer, wherever they were, in whatever part of the UK, similar themes come up time and time again. They thought they were the only ones, at first. They thought they'd have to hide certain parts of themselves, forever, or else mould themselves into versions that made others more at ease with their own selves. Boyfriends. Teddy bears on Valentine's Day. Bickering through Homebase. Engagements and joint social-media posts about it, 512 likes. A nice femme body encased in nice femme clothes. Babies. Death. These are the pressures that get piled onto women generally, regardless of sexuality. But for queer people they can feel especially alien, especially absurd, because so much of modern society is built around heterormative ideals. They're entrenched. Which means queerness requires a process of re-evaluating and undoing everything from the ground up. *Who are you and what is it you really want? Is it this, or is it something else?* Listen to your bones.

I cannot overstate the value of nightlife for queer people when it comes to this process. Nightlife shows you that there's another way. Whether you're swirling your tongue around the mouth of some genderless green-haired queer on the dancefloor with no one caring because they're too busy trying to hook up with their mates, or dancing to the A-Trak remix of 'Heads Will Roll' without the constant anticipation that some dude might try to grind up behind you, queer nights can act as parallel universes, temporary utopias, devoid of the expectations that cling to you like seaweed as soon as you exit the doors and the sun rises; face crumpled, soul radiant.

It's been over a decade since I first walked into The Joiners, but still I remember the feeling of being surrounded by queer people and still I crave that feeling today. I breathe a sigh of relief when I'm in an LGBTQ space, even now. It's subtle, my body relaxing in minute and indeterminable ways, like how your muscles stop tensing one by one when you climb into a hot bath.

When I ask Flo why lesbian and bi nightlife is still important, she puts it simply, in a way I'd imagine many of us can relate to: 'Even though we've got Tinder these days and it's never been easier to find a shag, nothing beats looking around a room and being in the majority. Not feeling like the odd one out, but feeling surrounded by your tribe,' she says. She pauses, then continues, 'And because raw female sexuality, that has nothing to do with men, is really fucking hot.'

CHAPTER FOUR

Pop Music

E lena Kiper had been having tooth troubles. Pain, constantly. The kind of pain that meant she couldn't concentrate on anything else – just the black, throbbing pressure, burrowed inside her gum. If it had been a sound it would have been a low and furious hum, eradicating all other sounds, like a vacuum.

Eventually Elena, who was around twenty-four years old and living in Russia at the time, agreed to have surgery to fix whatever it was that had been causing the pain. Once there, the dentist administered an oral sedative – Triazolam, Diazepam? – and she fell swiftly into a lucid slumber, head lolling on the dentist's chair, mouth wide open and drooling.

Elena's dreams were strange, wild, unusual – the sort of colourful half-dreams that can only be induced by chemicals. And among the swirl of her dream world, she found herself kissing another woman. She'd never thought about another woman in that way – at least not overtly. She'd always had boyfriends. But the dream-woman's lips were so soft and sweet, and the kiss was so slow . . .

'Я сошла с ума!' she exclaimed out loud, suddenly, waking herself up on the dentist's chair. 'I've lost my mind!' The dentist looked at her, only mildly puzzled – he was used to patients saying weird things while the sedatives wore off. Just last week a guy had woken himself up singing nursery rhymes. So when Elena left the surgery – eyes glazed, mouth still a little numb, tooth no longer throbbing – the dentist cleaned up his instruments, brewed a coffee and didn't think any more about it.

But Elena thought about it constantly. Not about the dream so much, but about that one phrase in relation to it: *I've lost my mind, I've lost my mind, I've lost my mind.* When she got home, she told her then-lover and business partner, Ivan Shapovalov (both of them were songwriters and producers), and they quickly tried weaving it into a song, adding new lines here and there, shaping a vague lesbian storyline: 'Mom they're looking at me/ Tell me what do you see?/Yes, I've lost my mind.'

Soon afterwards, the song had a name: 'All the Things She Said', and, in August 2002, was released as the debut single by the teenage Russian duo t.A.T.u.

That's one version of what's rumoured to have happened anyway. Who knows what really went down." Reports at the time made out that the idea for 'All the Things She Said' was initially Ivan's, while official writing credits cite a joint effort between Elena Kiper, Sergio Galoyan, Martin Kierszenbaum, Valery Polienko and Trevor Horn. Either way, 'All the Things She Said' went on to sell millions globally, becoming certified gold in seven different countries and platinum in five. In the UK, the track was number one for four consecutive weeks, and stayed in the charts for a further fifteen weeks. And within a year, t.A.T.u had won an MTV Video Music Award and were being invited to perform on talk shows across America: *The Tonight Show with Jay Leno, Last Call With Carson Daly, Jimmy Kimmel Live!*

It's easy to see why the song was such an immediate and monstrous success. It has all the camp, euro-club catchiness of

Cher's 'Believe' mashed up with the industrial beats and nu-metal riffs of a band like Evanescence, with a cold Russian twist. Singing along to it feels inevitable. The slow, sugary build-up. The heavy, high-drama chorus. The spiky walls of synth. It's hard to conceive of a more audacious combination of lyrics and production crammed into the space of three minutes and forty-eight seconds. Even now, two decades later, it still sounds moreish, delicious, like salty fast food washed down with sweet fizzy drinks.

From the very beginning, t.A.T.u – comprised of Lena Katina and Julia Volkova, seventeen and eighteen at the time – were marketed as a young lesbian couple. In photos they would hold hands, and even their name is reportedly a play on the Russian phrase '*Та любит Ту*', meaning 'This girl loves that one'. The lyrics to 'All the Things She Said' are unambiguously about forbidden same-sex desire, as per Elena's dream: 'When they stop and stare, don't worry me/Cause I'm feeling for her what she's feeling for me.'

The video, directed by Ivan Shapovalov and shot in Moscow, cemented their image as schoolgirls in love. Lena and Julia sing in the rain beneath a thunderous green sky, hands clasped around metal bars, Catholic uniforms soaked, before leaning in for a kiss just as the song reaches its crescendo: 'This is not enough/This is not enough.' The video was played repeatedly on The Box, MTV and The Hit, becoming as locked into everyone's minds as the idea had been in Elena's that day at the dentist's. Every time you switched on the TV, there they were: Uniforms. Pouring rain. Snogging. Repeat.

All of this might have been progressive, radical even, had Lena and Julia been a real same-sex couple, even more so had they come up with the song themselves. Especially considering the band had come out of Russia, a country notorious for its anti-LGBTQ laws and attitudes. But in a 2003 documentary, *Ta-Ta t.A.T.u*, both confirmed that they weren't with each other, and, in fact, had long-term boyfriends. Julia later came out as bisexual, while Lena said she was straight. But regardless of what genders they were into, queerness had been used as a marketing tool for the band by a team behind the scenes. The duo had been put together and advised to make out with each other in order to sell records. And, lo and behold, it had worked.

T.A.T.u, of course, caused outrage from the off. But viewers weren't too bothered about the duo being performatively queer in order to make money for old men while actual queer women were being subjugated within the industry and rarely given airtime. They were more bothered about the lesbian stuff. TV presenters Richard and Judy campaigned to have the music video banned for 'pandering to paedophiles', despite the fact equally raunchy heterocentric displays were everywhere. (Britney Spears had already become an international megastar, helped in part by her 1998 breakout hit '. . . Baby One More Time', in the video for which she plays a Catholic school girl longing for her boyfriend.) ITV banned the t.A.T.u video from *CD:UK* because it 'wasn't suitable for children' (again, the entire 1980s and 1990s had already happened, featuring Madonna simulating bondage play and group sex in her videos). The BBC denied banning the music video from *Top of the Pops*, although it seems weird they never played it, considering it was literally the only song people were buying for weeks.

As a young queer kid, I don't remember caring or even thinking about whether t.A.T.u were real lesbians or not. Nobody was real anything in music videos; that was the point wasn't it? On the flipside, I don't remember the kiss between them changing my life either. I just liked the song because it was catchy. But for a lot of queer viewers, 'All the Things She Said' marked a sexual awakening of sorts. They'd never seen two girls make out on TV like this before, and now they were everywhere and just a few years older than them, like the cool girls at school but gayer and drenched in rain. Who cared if they had boyfriends? They weren't here right now, were they?

'I was so obsessed with them, I watched their videos on repeat constantly. I was so young that I don't think I cared that it was all fake, all I cared about was that they were hot,' twenty-nine-year-old Sarah tells me. 'I didn't know the backstory, I was far too distracted by the kissing and the rain,' says twenty-seven-year-old Ruby E. Twenty-seven-year-old Sadhbh feels similarly: 'It was one hundred per cent my sexual awakening. I didn't even know why I loved it so much, I just remember sitting as close to the TV as possible when they were on. I would watch the parody of *Cruel Intentions* in *Not Another Teen Movie* when I was fifteen, and then actual *Cruel Intentions* when I was sixteen. I fucking loved these performative straight girl kisses.'

Had t.A.T.u emerged fifteen or even ten years later, their impact might have been felt differently, their faux-queerness viewed as appropriative, the well-oiled money machine behind them recognised as problematic. When Rita Ora released 'Girls' in 2018, for instance, alongside Cardi B, Bebe Rexha and Charli XCX, the pop star faced a widespread backlash for her portrayal of same-sex relationships. With lyrics about hooking up with girls after drinking red wine and how 'Last night, yeah, we got with a dude/I saw him, he was lookin' at you', the song was criticised for invalidating real queer feelings, for exacerbating the stereotype that girls only get off with each other when trashed or wanting some guy's attention. Rita Ora was then forced to justify her own queerness in a public apology, which many viewed as a misplaced form of retribution. Why should audiences be the ones to police anyone's expression of their queerness, as relating to their own experiences? But equally, had pop culture not moved on?

When t.A.T.u emerged, none of these conversations were happening. At least not in the way they are now, in the public sphere, on our phones and timelines, a constant back-and-forth buzz. Katy Perry's 'I Kissed a Girl' was still six years into the future. Madonna, Britney Spears and Christina Aguilera had yet to swirl tongues onstage at the 2003 MTV Video Music Awards, in a performance so unabashedly camp, so deliciously absurd in its homage to (or appropriation of) queer aesthetics, that you would have to be devoid of delight not to enjoy it. In other words, t.A.T.u's legacy today exists in two separate lanes. As an iconic moment for the queers. And as a totem for how rare it was to see queerness depicted in mainstream pop, and how it was even rarer to see it from artists who were queer themselves.

§

Queer women have long held a complicated place in mainstream music. In part because 'queerness' in art – the expression and absorption of it – has always been difficult to quantify. And in part because queer women have often been left out of that conversation anyway. Ask the average person on the street about queer women in music before the mid-1990s and they'd probably be hard-pressed to think of artists beyond k.d. lang, Tracy Chapman and Melissa Etheridge. Folk musicians singing softly and earnestly – though rarely explicitly sexually – about yearning. As critic Jodie Taylor noted in her 2013 essay 'Lesbian Musicalities, Queer Strains and Celesbian Pop': 'In terms of both gender and genre, lesbian music often evokes a kind of mainstream ordinariness, suggesting melancholy confessionals sung by dowdy androgynous women strumming acoustic guitars.'

That's not all there was, obviously. Like other LGBTQ artists, lesbian and bi people people carved spaces for themselves outside of the mainstream, creating their own kind of subcultures, either because they had to or they wanted to. The rise of queercore in the 1980s and 1990s, for instance, indicated a dissatisfaction with not only heteronormative society, but also with the gay liberation movement, which appeared to place gay middle-class white men at the top and queer women of colour, transgender, intersex and genderqueer folk below. Queercore also stood to the left of punk and even riot grrrl. Bands like Fifth Column, Tribe 8, Team Dresch, The Third Sex, The Need and Sister George – who were, to borrow the words of 'terrorist drag' icon Vaginal Davis, 'too gay for the punks and too punk for the gays' – sprang out of Olympia, San Francisco, Portland, Toronto and London, creating scenes for young lesbian and bi people to recognise themselves within, a community to be part of. This isn't to say that queercore was always potently revolutionary – in many instances the scene fell victim to the same limitations as riot grrrl, becoming a genre dominated by white faces and spaces – but many viewed the genre as sticking a middle finger up to gay assimilation. As queercore founder Bruce LaBruce told *Dazed* in 2016, 'We were fighting the gay mainstream by promoting no division between gays and lesbians, by being inclusive of queers of all races, ages, genders and sexual persuasions.'

Listening to queercore bands in the 1990s talk about lesbian and bi representation in music sounds remarkably similar to bands having similar conversations today: 'There are always going to be queers,' says Leslie Mah from Tribe 8 in the 1997 documentary *She's Real (Worse than Queer)* by Lucy Thane, her San Franciscan drawl floating through the blurry VHS. 'It would have made all the difference in the world to me had there been an "out" band at that time when I was sixteen. Or even for bands to say they're queer positive. To even be acknowledged as a person who takes up space. So when we play, it's like "Yeah I want the dykes to take up all the space in this club".

'Historically, whenever homosexuality gets talked about, it's gay men that are being talked about. Lesbians have been completely invisiblised and are considered non-sexual creatures; like basically you're a lesbian because you're asexual, you're impotent, you can't fuck . . .' says Tammy Rae Carland, a prominent riot grrrl photographer and lesbian record-label owner, in that same film. 'It's like people saying "we don't need any more love songs". Well maybe you don't. But I do. I don't have enough love songs for my experience. I don't have enough girl heroes in my face.'

But with song names like 'Fagetarian and Dyke' (Team Dresch) and 'Rim Me Isabella' (The Need), or live shows depicting strap-on blow jobs, bloody tampons and bondage (Tribe 8), queercore bands weren't exactly reaching mainstream television. They didn't even reach the mainstream press, although most of them, of course, didn't want to. Instead, DIY zines were made and distributed among the community in an effort to keep the message of their music alive, their history intact, without being filtered through a conformist lens. As Camille Erickson wrote in her 2013 essay 'Querying Sex, Gender, and Race through the Queercore Zine Movement', 'Self-identified queercore artists adamantly objected to the assimilation of queer culture into the mainstream. The zines, by documenting and reclaiming the queer body, launched a collective space for queer people to imagine and live alternative identities outside mainstream society.'

'A lot of us had to educate ourselves . . . we didn't know what had gone on before, and that's part of the problem because we're repeating the same kind of arguments,' says Miriam Basilio, an art historian and queercore fan in *She's Real (Worse than Queer)*, 'and that's what the dominant culture wants, they want us not to be informed and for us not to have a history for ourselves.'

While all of this was happening – in sweaty basements, behind grainy Super 8 lenses, hand-scrawled onto zines – mainstream music remained predictably untouched by the queer underground, regardless of what part of the world you lived in, initially at least. By the tail-end of the 1990s, UK music in particular had become enamoured with a kind of brazen heterosexualism. On one end you had the deliriously straight bubblegum pop of the Spice Girls, Steps and 5ive, and on the other were a slew of Britpop blokes like Oasis, Blur and others people would barely remember later, like Babylon Zoo, Cornershop and Fat Les. And while there were a few notable exceptions – Brian Molko from Placebo being one of them; a bisexual man who to me felt like a lesbian crush, Skin from Skunk Anansie being another – queerness in the mainstream was distant, rare, lost among a sea of sweaty-fringed lads in bucket hats and polo shirts, fist pumping with one hand and chanting 'Lager! Lager! Lager!' while swilling beer around with the other.

§

This was the context in which t.A.T.u were received just a handful of years later. Positive attitudes towards LGBTQ people might have been at an all-time high compared to previous decades, but in the early 2000s it was still rare to see 'out' queer women in mainstream pop, or on primetime television, especially in ways that deviated from femme-presenting cisgender skinny white girls making out for an ever-present male gaze.

As the decade wore on, the indie world made way for a few exceptions. Peaches, Le Tigre, Tegan and Sara, The Gossip. When Beth Ditto appeared on the cover of *NME* in 2007, naked and with a flash of armpit hair alongside the caption 'Kiss My Ass', it felt like a significant cultural moment. Here was a fat queer woman in a power pose on the front of the UK's most circulated music magazine. 'I love naked Beth Ditto on the cover of *NME*! Genius!' gushed Courtney Love in a blog post at the time, 'Best *NME* cover since PJ Harvey in the chicken yard by Anton Corbijn.' But the following week at *NME*, it was back to The White Stripes and then Muse followed by Johnny Borrell. In fact, when you look at all fifty-one *NME* covers from 2007, only three women make an appearance: Beth Ditto, Meg White from The White Stripes and Kate Nash. The rest are white men, with the exception of James Brown following his death and two covers dedicated to Bloc Party. It was as if women – very occasionally queer women – could have their moment as a treat, but only as a brief deviation from the norm, as a way for brands to show how edgy they were before going back to a more comfortable status quo.

When I speak to lesbian and bi music fans about this era, many say a similar thing, mention the same few bands. 'I don't remember many queer women in pop then, but Beth Ditto from The Gossip was major in terms of seeing someone who was openly queer and also successful in a way that wasn't necessarily related to her queerness,' one music fan tells me. 'As a Black lesbian in my teens there was no one who looked like me on TV or even in magazines,' says another, 'but I got really into Peaches because she didn't give a fuck, and more tomboyish hip hop artists with what you might call a "gay aesthetic". Lil' Kim, TLC, Missy Elliott . . . they were all major for me in a lot of ways.'

Laura Snapes, now deputy music editor at the *Guardian*, remembers how there was a major drought of openly queer women artists at the time. She would trawl through message boards dedicated to the 2003 *Fame Academy* winner Alex Parks (a lesbian musician from Cornwall who has since disappeared entirely from public life) in the hopes of finding some equally queer recommendations. She discovered the punk pop duo Tegan and Sara that way, she says, and immediately went to the CD shop in town to buy their third album, *If It Was You*. 'My best friend and I sat on my bedroom floor with our backs up against my single bed, and played it,' Laura tells me. 'Then I became fully obsessed. I used all my lunch breaks at school to go into the IT room and read about them and look at pictures of them online.'

Laura didn't get into Tegan and Sara because of their queerness, per se, but it was definitely a 'key element'. 'If you were into Avril Lavigne or Paramore or anything pop punk related on MTV, Tegan and Sara were really not that far from something like that. So I think I'd have liked them anyway. But I don't think I'd have been exposed to them had I not gone looking for something like that in the first place.' It wasn't as if queer women were getting loads of airtime outside of queer-focused community spaces.

One of my favourite artists from this very same era was the synth-pop musician Ladyhawke, whose real name is Pip Brown. I remember finding tracks of hers on MySpace – 'Back of the Van', 'Paris is Burning' – and being taken aback by this woman with shaggy Stevie Nicks hair, who seemed to love her guitar and synth in equal measure, playing this cool, almost sensual 1980s electro-pop with an indie rock edge. I didn't know she was gay back then because she didn't speak about it, but when she released her track 'My Delirium' it *felt* like a gay track in a way that's difficult to explain. A friend of mine put it best recently when she described the chorus, the bit when Ladyhawke shouts 'Hey!', as sounding like 'the moment a really fit lesbian pushes you against the wall on a dancefloor'.

But Ladyhawke didn't 'make sense' alongside other musicians that were around at the time. Or at least that's how she was made to feel. She'd just moved to London from a small town in New Zealand, and was inexplicably being lumped in with La Roux, Florence and the Machine, and Little Boots by the mainstream music press – artists who didn't resemble her sonically or visually – just because she was a woman. She was openly gay in her personal life and has been since the age of twenty-one. But when her music started gaining traction, and she then went on to release her acclaimed self-titled debut album through Modular Recordings in 2008, she was made to keep this aspect of herself private.

'It became apparent to me that all the people in power, all these male gatekeepers, didn't want me to be gay,' Pip tells me. 'I was told by multiple people – labels, management – not to tell anyone. It was really hard for me because I never hid my sexuality from anybody. I brought my girlfriend at the time with me everywhere. When I first started as Ladyhawke, I'd been working on my music for ages without even a question of whether my sexuality was going to be an issue. And then arriving in the UK and getting all the buzz that I got . . . I basically got told to shut up, to not talk about it, to not tell anyone because it would ruin my career.'

Homophobia and misogyny aren't always so overt. Attitudes bleed into day-to-day interactions in more insidious ways. In glances and hesitations and words unsaid. In being subtly pushed to be a certain way, made to feel 'wrong' about how you comfortably present. This is also what Pip experienced at the height of her success, at a time in which she was appearing in *NME* and on multiple 'cool' lists. 'Nobody knew what to do with me,' she remembers. (One 2008 album review in *Pitchfork* literally reads, 'Part of the problem might be that no one really knows what to make of her.') 'I would turn up to photoshoots and the stylist would always try and put me in clothes I didn't want to wear,' she says. 'That's been a massive thing in my life. I don't like wearing heels or dresses, it makes me feel like I'm . . . it makes me feel like I want to cry, that's the only way to describe it. It's not me and it makes me feel really yucky. So that was something I always struggled with as well; how people wanted me to look, as opposed to how I wanted to look.'

This took an enormous toll on Pip's mental health and the trauma seeped into her creative process. On the phone she's open and relaxed, laughing often, but I can tell it's not an easy era to look back on. 'I was really angry, I can't express how angry I was. They wanted me to get to work straight away on another record and I wasn't ready. I was like, "I'm not going to make the record you want, I'm in a dark place, I'm going to go away and make the darkest possible record I can make." That first record came from pure innocence and joy and happiness and my second record, *Anxiety*, was a fuck-you to everyone.' She pauses, breathes in. 'My drinking was out of control at that point. I was constantly drinking and taking pills. I was just not in a good place. That part of my life has forever damaged me.'

Pip has since got sober, moved back to New Zealand and had a baby with her wife, Madeleine. In 2016 she released a third album, *Wild Things*, a brilliant sparkling record crammed with smooth shiny synth and hyper-clean vocals, this time through Mid Century Records in Europe and Polyvinyl in the United States. During the release cycle she was able to be open about exactly who she is. But it's eye-opening talking to her about how different the situation was behind the scenes just ten or fifteen years ago. While PRs, labels and managers are now eager to flaunt an artist's queerness in a way that borderlines commodifying, it really wasn't so long ago that those same groups of people were telling their artists to keep hush hush about their orientation or gender identity, just in case it affected the influx of money.

'I'm so glad it's sort of changed so dramatically in even just the last three years,' Pip says. 'The change is so massive, and it's so exciting and important seeing how accepting the world is now of everything – age, gender, queerness – that's what makes me keep going.'

§

It's difficult to pinpoint the moment queer women became more visible in mainstream music. Progress is never linear and pop culture evolves in a multitude of contradictory ways. The mid-2010s ushered in a new era for queer representation. Queer kids in the 2000s might have been gluing themselves to MTV in the hope of catching two Russian teenagers graze lips for 0.2 seconds in the rain, but fifteen years later and all the next generation needed to do was go on YouTube and search for any number of major pop videos.

Today queer women are everywhere – or at least that's how it feels in comparison to a decade or so ago. We have US artists like Halsey, Demi Lovato, Kehlani, Miley Cyrus and Janelle Monáe improving bisexual and pansexual representation. Pop stars like Hayley Kiyoko and Shura actually using the word 'lesbian' in reference to themselves (Kiyoko, whose videos rack up around 100 million views on YouTube, has been nicknamed 'Lesbian Jesus' by her young fans). Rappers like Angel Haze, Azealia Banks and Young M.A. owning their queerness in a way that feels incidental, non-sensationalist. Critically acclaimed artists like St. Vincent, Syd, and Christine and the Queens making music about woman-to-woman love and sex. And King Princess – a twenty-something-year-old openly gay musician – appearing in *Playboy* shoots wearing American football shoulder pads and little else, waved hair slick with sweat, like a sort of soft butch genderqueer pin-up for Gen Z.

None of this happened overnight. Dr Kristin J. Lieb, author of *Gender, Branding, and The Modern Music Industry*, tells me that a few things happened simultaneously in the lead-up to this significant shift. Lady Gaga coming out as bisexual in 2009, for instance, was pivotal in terms of seeing queerness in mainstream pop that wasn't strictly performative for a male gaze, as per the Madonna/Britney/Christina VMAs kiss or Katy Perry's 'I Kissed a Girl'. A year after coming out, Gaga then released her music video to 'Telephone', in which she gets marched into prison by two female guards and wrapped in chains. In the prison yard, a high butch, androgynous prisoner in a leather waistcoat – played by trans masc performance artist Heather Cassils – wordlessly leans in for a kiss, muscles rippling. It's titillating, sure, but titillating for who? Here we can see the tide turning – queer desire for a queer gaze – immeasurable at first, but unquestionably there.

Meanwhile, the world was continuing to change. In the early 2010s, LGBTQ rights were suddenly up for mainstream debate in the UK and US. In 2010, the US government lifted their 'Don't Ask, Don't Tell' policy, meaning that openly gay, lesbian and bisexual people could serve in all branches of the military. That same year, the UK introduced the Equality Act 2010, meaning that it was unlawful to discriminate against anyone based on their sexual orientation. In 2013, same-sex marriage became legalised across England and Wales, coming into force on

13 March 2014. And two years later, under President Obama, the US followed suit, lifting the ban on same-sex marriage in all fifty states. In other words, while queer culture has often existed separately – and sometimes in direct opposition to – heteronormative structures, it makes sense that socially progressive politics would have a knock-on effect in relation to where queer art exists within in the Western mainstream. Not only because laws validate attitudes and attitudes shape culture, but because when your essential rights are suddenly subject to negotiation, there's an urgency that permeates the queer existence: *Whose side are you on? How long will this last? Do I need to be louder?*

Around this time, musicians were being increasingly vocal about both their own identities and where they stood on the political scale. Miley Cyrus, for instance – an artist from a country background who first shot to fame on the Disney Channel as wholesome all-American character Hannah Montana – came out as pansexual in 2015. During that same year, she launched the Happy Hippie Foundation, a non-profit organisation that aims to provide homeless LGBTQ youth with support and prevention services. To raise money for the charity, she performed duets with various artists in her backyard for YouTube, including a cover of 'Androgynous' by The Replacements with trans singer Laura Jane Grace and Joan Jett (an artist who has never apparently come out, but who remains a queer icon nonetheless). This might seem like a drop in the ocean in comparison to LGBTQ activists of decades prior, whose bodies and livelihoods were literally at risk for taking up space. But for an artist like Miley – who epitomises the American mainstream, whose videos get millions upon millions of views – to stand by queer rights and to elevate queer voices felt emblematic in relation to where the general mood was heading.

MUNA, a queer synth-pop trio from Los Angeles, made use of this cultural moment. 'I think scholars will look back on that period of time – the transition between the Obama administration and the legalisation of gay marriage and the mainstreaming of shows like *Modern Family* and then the onset of the Trump administration – as being the kick in the ass to a lot of queer creative people to be openly out and to more radically embrace their identities across the board,' explains Naomi, guitarist and producer in MUNA. The trio were initially wary about being pigeon-holed as a queer band but they've since become known for their huge legion of devoted queer women and non-binary fans ('Sad soft pop songs for sissies, angry girls, emo queers and crybabies', reads their merch.) I've heard MUNA being referred to as 'The Queer Haim' – a description that is probably a disservice to the originality of both acts, but sort of makes sense as a sonic comparison.

MUNA's singer Katie agrees: 'A lot of our success as a band can be attributed to timing. I think it was 2014, and we thought that there were queer people with enough power; if we owned that part of ourselves, people would come out and support us and give us a platform,' she says. 'But it was way more than we expected . . . I don't know if there's a name for this, but there was a queer whirlwind. And all of a sudden, it was so much more in the mainstream within less than a year.'

'There was a lot of great pop music that came out of the early 2000s,' Naomi continues. 'But I think we grew up in a very unfortunate time in terms of where culture was with the queer community, where culture was visually in terms of gender performance and with body image – we kind of got the shit end of the stick. I felt very stifled by mainstream culture as a young teen. We just live in a completely different time now. I feel like the kids who are growing up now are so much more aware of the spectrum of gender identities and performance and sexual identities and all that stuff. I'm happy to be making music right now.'

I've seen MUNA perform a bunch of times and can probably recite most of their lyrics. One summer in the late 2010s, two friends and I spent a couple of weeks driving around LA, loudly singing along to their first album blaring from the car speakers. I can still remember the feeling: the specific smell of Hollywood that can only be described as palm tree wood, hot dirt and sweet perfume. The flat yellow sunshine holding my face through the window. My friends and I screaming the lyrics to each other but also to ourselves, well aware of the absurdity of singing such sad, tragic words in such a glittering, pleasureful place.

We had all been through, or were going through, heartbreak in one way or another. I was in love with someone who I wasn't sure loved me back. And here I was in my favourite place on Earth with my two of my favourite people – winding through dusty hillsides, stumbling drunk through Trader Joe's at night-time for snacks, smoking cigarettes on the roof at sunrise – but still, parts of me were hurting. We had come here for an escape, all of us. And we sang the most overly dramatic, most unapologetic of the MUNA lyrics, constantly, well aware of how saccharine and on-the-nose we sounded: "Cause the world could be burning, and all I'd be thinking is "How are you doing, baby?" '

When MUNA's second album, *Saves The World,* came out in 2019, those same friends and I went to see them play at Shepherd's Bush Empire in west London. Things were different by that point, I was less miserable, my life having taken a neater and more comfortable turn. But their music still tapped into a specific type of queer longing that I recognised; a melodrama wrapped up in desire just out of reach, encouraging listeners to encase themselves in difficult emotions and dance through the pain. And in that venue, I felt peaceful. An old ex and her new fiancée were somewhere behind me, leaning on each other in the dark. They looked good together. We were wearing cowboy hats and vests. Everywhere you turned there were young lesbians and queer kids, screaming, elated on their own history, high on their own eternal heartbreak: 'I'm gonna die alone/In my bedroom/ Looking at strangers on my telephone.'

I'm curious as to whether MUNA think female queerness in particular has a pop sound. I often think it does, but have found it hard to describe. 'I've been having some conversations recently, talking about the history of the themes of yearning and unrequited love in queer music,' Katie considers. 'And that solves the question of why there's such an extensive history of gay men being the core fanbase of certain straight women, certain pop stars and the narratives that they have. I think Robyn makes queer music because a lot of her music is about heartbreak and unrequited love and shame. "Shame" is the big word that nobody wants to include in the conversation of what a lot of pop songs are about. But I think it's fair to say they are.'

It's hard to imagine a band like MUNA existing before now – or at least having the same sort of platform. We may have had Tegan and Sara – the closest, perhaps, in terms of audience and level of queer representation – but to have a major-label-backed pop band releasing songs overtly about lesbian and bi relationships in a way that feels authentic is something that feels distinct to this era. When Harry Styles asked them to open for his 2017 solo tour across Europe and North America, this culture shift was underlined. Here was a then relatively unknown queer trio bringing their sound to one of the most highly publicised tours at the time, alongside an ex-boy-band member with a legion of devoted followers. It's difficult to envision the same situation happening with Robbie Williams back in the day, for instance, or Justin Timberlake, when queerness among women was considered the thing that haemorrhaged money rather than multiplied it (based, I'd imagine, on the old assumption that audiences have no interest in narratives that fail to centre men, nor queerness outside of sexual props). Next time, maybe a queer band won't need support from a male artist in order to play stadiums.

MUNA remain simultaneously happy and sceptical when it comes to the mainstreaming of queerness and their place within that conversation. 'I think it's an ongoing concept that we have to negotiate,' considers Naomi. 'We are obviously very fortunate and incredibly honoured to be part of an amazing community, at such an amazing time, and be able to make a living from making pop music while being who we are. But at the same time, I think we're all very conscious that the power structures that be have a very devious way of putting their thing down, flipping and reversing the whole situation.

'They do that with all marginalised communities; they absorb them into the mainstream and then figure out a way to sell it and deradicalise it. That is something that is constantly happening. We talk about the corporatisation of Pride a lot when that comes around. So yeah, there's a sort of dual happiness and disappointment when it comes to the way it all shakes down.'

§

Queer representation in music is something I didn't realise I needed until it was there – or at least until there was more of it. Young people absorb pop culture, they pocket away its subtle messaging and inherit its version of the truth. They seek to find reflections of themselves, feelings that resemble theirs, iconography to aspire to. Because before you go out and seek IRL communities, that's all there is: words and images on screens, songs in headphones, real human emotions like desire and love and heartbreak melded into neatly formed packages to be consumed and then used as the lens in which you view the world and your place within it.

As a kid in the 1990s and 2000s, I never looked around and thought, 'this is really heteronormative.' Even if I'd had that sort of language to explain things, lack of representation encroaches in more cunning ways. Instead, I saw Britney Spears with her toned glossy stomach and pigtails, longing for a boyfriend in the corridors at school, while a queer version remained unimaginable. I sang along with the Spice Girls' '2 Become 1': 'Any deal that we endeavour/Boys and girls feel good together.' I plugged myself into third-wave emo songs, the ones in which girls are a nameless force, a destructive absence, identified only by the pain caused to whichever boy happens to be screaming. And in doing so subconsciously absorbed the idea that women were lesser, that queer women were invisible, or else, sexual props for men and that these skewed narratives represented truth.

Seeing queerness in pop that speaks to the queer women gaze – St. Vincent in sugar-pink latex purring, 'I don't turn off what turns me on', Christine and the Queens sucking Caroline Polachek's neck in 'La Vita Nuova', Syd visibly comfortable in her butchness – has a way of legitimising certain versions of desire and the presentation of such desire. When I think back to how I was feeling as a young teen still cloudy about her sexuality – more interested in watching a woman paint her nails than having a boy's hand scrambling around in my bra – I realise that queer desire was, to me and to many, a private conversation, an internal battle. To have those private conversations turned public, normalised, scrubbed from shame, does wonders to the way queer people move throughout the world.

This isn't to say that queer people can't and don't identify themselves within love/sex/heartbreak songs by straight artists, or vice versa – we do constantly. Feelings produced by music are often fluid and complicated and genderless; sometimes you are the ex-lover Prince is singing about in 'Nothing Compares 2 U', sometimes you are Prince himself. But mostly you are the shades of purple in between; the line 'It's been seven hours and fifteen days', the moment Prince's voice breaks in the second to last verse. But it's worth acknowledging what heteronormativity can do to the queer psyche and celebrating an alternative. When you are constantly positioned within the mainstream as either invisible or 'the other', it is easy to feel as if your experiences are somehow abnormal or simply not there. *I can't see myself anywhere, so the problem must be me.*

For queer people of colour, these barriers have always been heightened. During the 2000s' fauxmosexuality boom, the women who were flirting with queerness in pop were predominately white, cisgender and conventionally femme. But as writer and activist Reeta Loi points out in a 2019 issue of *Gay Times*, the later wave of queer women in pop look a lot different to a decade ago. 'Why is the explosion of queer women in music overwhelmingly led by women of colour?' she asks, namechecking artists like Janelle Monáe, Syd, Hayley Kiyoko and Rina Sawayama. 'Because our intersections have power and, perhaps, we're realising that the more intersections we live at, the more power we have. To elaborate; the more marginalised groups we embody, the more opportunity we have to explore the breadth of life, which is the artist's obsession: to experience and to feel.'

On the phone, Dr Kristin J. Lieb – the theorist and author – also mentions how the queer women dominating pop's mainstream today look a lot different to those we remember from the past. We're not just seeing more queer women, we're seeing more queer women of colour, plus those who don't necessarily fit within a gender binary (although it's worth pointing out here that non-binary visibility in mainstream music is still relatively new and also woefully thin on ground). 'The only time that we've even had a moment that looked anything like this was in the late 1980s and early 1990s when we had k.d. lang and Melissa Etheridge and the Indigo Girls alongside riot grrrl,' she says. 'But that was almost completely white, so it looks completely different today. We have a much richer and more inclusive representational moment.'

None of this is to say that we are living in a perfect, utopian juncture – far from it. Queerness among women is still being used as a marketing tool, as it was when t.A.T.u were advised to make out with each other to sell records for straight guys in power (the wealth never seeming to reach queer women themselves). But this time the vibe is different. Queerness isn't necessarily positioned as being titillating for an imagined male gaze: two girls in soaked school uniforms desperate to get closer, Katy Perry eyeing the camera while singing about how a girl's lips tasted like cherry Chapstick. Instead, authentic queerness has become cool. It's become the thing that makes an artist stand out from their peers. 'NEW TRACK FROM QUEER SINGER' reads the subject line in emails I get from music PRs while working as a journalist; 'XYZ COMES OUT AS GENDERFLUID!' Queerness is still being used to make money, but the angle has shifted. It's about *how queer* you are, how political you are in that queerness and how you as an artist are personally moving the conversation forward.

This new embrace of queerness in pop culture can lean dangerously close to tokenisation and pinkwashing, as well as expecting more from our queer artists than their straight coun-terparts. Oftentimes, it can be difficult to differentiate between real, tangible progression, and capitalist motives under the guise of it. This is, after all, the era of Marks and Spencer's LGBT Pride sandwiches, of Listerine's rainbow-coloured mouthwash, of the Home Office changing its social-media profile picture to the colours of the Pride flag during a time in which 78 per cent of asylum cases from LGBTQ applicants are turned down. Speaking about progression when it comes to queerness in pop is complex; just because queerness is having a public moment, doesn't mean that all queer people from all backgrounds are benefitting.

Heightened awareness of pinkwashing and tokenisation has caused the queer community to keep a wary eye on what constitutes real representation. This frustration can sometimes spill over into policing and gatekeeping each other. 'The thing that is freaking me out is that now we're dividing from within about what counts as authentic queer representation,' says Kristen. 'We're saying things like "Rita Ora isn't really queer". When representation is scarce, people are like, "Well, she didn't do this and this and this" . . . She can't embody every idea about being queer; if you made a character like that everyone would hate her because she'd be so artificial.

'We're expecting pop stars to have PhDs in gender and sexuality studies. People who have studied those subjects might have more nuanced takes on things, but pop stars are often just young people trying to figure out their identity,' Kristen continues. 'So why are we pitting these pop stars against each other? There's room for everyone. Representationally, why can't we be okay with having a wide range of what "being queer" looks like? My fear is that if we make it so uncomfortable for people to be out and queer in their own way, whatever that means to them personally, then we're going to come back to a place where we only have a few people representing us.' I hear what Kristen is saying. And while she's saying it, I also wonder how much of this in-fighting largely benefits the oppressor: if we're so busy debating each other, how will we ever find the time, organisation and actual energy to dismantle heternormative systems?

In an era where queer artists are expected to shout about their queerness, some also feel uncomfortable about being defined by their sexuality in ways that straight artists are not. 'I think sometimes I get tired and bored of being on lists like "The Ten Best Queer Records of the Year",' Shura, an alt-pop artist from Manchester, tells me over coffee during a particularly bright spring morning. She's been out as gay from the start of her career and has garnered a loyal fanbase of young queer followers. ('I would say my audience is 50 per cent queer women,' she reels off proudly.) But she also just makes great pop music about love and sex and desire, and all the other complicated feelings that straight and queer people alike write about. 'Can I not just be in the one hundred top best records of the year? They don't have to be in the top ten . . . some people release better albums than I do.

'That said, I realise that that list isn't for me,' she considers. She'd rather be pigeon-holed as gay than culturally detach herself from the label entirely. There's always this sense of wishing to pay it forward, she says. 'The list of the ten best queer records is for fifteen-year-old queer kids googling "good queer records", doing the same thing that I was doing at home in my attic ten years ago. I guess it's necessary. We have to commodify it a bit for the gays who need to be able to discover music which will appeal to them in a different way.'

§

It's been two decades since t.A.T.u released 'All the Things She Said'. Listening to it now is nothing but a simple pleasure. What was once monumental, era-defining, has faded into pure millennial nostalgia. Drop it at 2 a.m. in a club full of dykes and the dancefloor will inevitably go wild. Those peach-soft vocals, that jagged mosh-pit synth, those emotive yet entirely nonsensical lyrics.

In some ways everything has changed since that song's release. We live in a largely altered world from the early 2000s. Ideas about the validity of the queer gaze in pop, ideas about the multitude of queer women artists that can exist in the same arena simultaneously, ideas about queer artists being given the space to make music that authentically speaks to their own experience, have shifted to such a degree that the premise of t.A.T.u seems faintly ridiculous now. *How were they even a thing?* you might ponder, when you take a step back for a moment, while also guiltily feeling pleased that they were.

But in other, more fundamental ways, the world isn't so different. We might appreciate significant culture shifts, and we might hope for even more significant cultural shifts in the future. But alongside that, most of us just want a banging track we can dance along to together. Something that lifts our insides. Something that makes us want to get closer to other bodies, something that makes us forget or embrace our own for a moment, something we can share.

CHAPTER FIVE

Part One: TV

It's the pilot of Showtime's 2010 reality show *The Real L Word*, and the cast members are recounting their very first sexual experience with a woman to the camera. Whitney Mixter, who at this point has dreads and is wearing an undone pinstripe bow-tie dangling around her neck, immediately marks herself out as an alpha character with an indefinable sort of charm. You can almost hear the lesbian hearts behind her, shattering.

'I'm nine, she's eleven and she's got boobs,' she begins, smiling slightly with an eyebrow raised, one leg casually balanced across the other. 'We're trying to be all romantic and sexy and I'm like, "Let me put whipped cream all over you and lick it." I didn't have whipped cream, but I did have sour cream, so I put sour cream on her boobs and thought, "To make it sweet I'll put fruity pebbles on it" then I proceeded to eat it off.'

Fast forward towards the end of the hour-long episode, and various lesbians and bi women are lingering outside an LA club. Some of them are arguing. Others are screaming. Everyone appears to be in ripped skinny jeans and have side fringes and are making each other jealous. 'I don't know why you make my heart hurt,' Whitney slurs, swaying beside some parked cars while twirling the hair of her new love interest Sada, who two seasons later becomes her wife, then eventually ex-wife. Then, before you know it, you're watching each of the cast members back in their different bedrooms in their various homes, hooking up with whomever they decided to bring back from the club. Tassel boots are kicked off, leather bracelets placed on nightstands and soft porn music *ta, ta, tas* gently in the background.

Despite the porno soundtrack, you don't see much action during that first episode: a bit of over-the-trousers straddling before the camera pans outside to the trees. But you can hear some panting, a few people moaning. It feels hilariously out of place, suddenly listening in on something so overtly sexual on an otherwise standardly formatted reality TV show – but this is lesbian TV, where the rules are different. Lesbian TV is trashier, famously so. 'You just made me come,' someone says in that weird, thick voice specifically reserved for chaotic sex at 4 a.m. after downing seven JD and Cokes and multiple shots of tequila. By the time the credits roll – after Whitney drives Sada to the airport the next morning and then, inexplicably, picks up a different, similar-looking girl on the same trip to take home straight afterwards – you're left wondering what the hell you just watched. Was it really reality television? An erotic docuseries? A lesbian comedy? And then, maybe, probably, you decide to watch some more.

The Real L Word launched immediately after the success of its older sister, the much loved and oft-referenced Showtime drama series *The L Word*. Both were produced by the same person, Ilene Chaiken, and while the former was American television's first-ever ensemble cast of lesbian and bisexual characters, the latter was basically the same but in real life. Aside from maybe MTV's long-running reality show *The Real World* (yeah I know, they all have similar sort of names), which included a few LGBTQ women over the years, this was the first time we'd seen the real lives of young queer women centred on screen.

Airing between 2010 and 2012 for three seasons, the show followed a group of lesbian and bi women in Los Angeles, San Francisco and New York as they fell out, made out, partied and tried to navigate complicated relationships and careers, all set to a backdrop of sleazy, late 2000s chick rock. The show had its drawbacks, obviously – it mostly depicted a narrow subsection of white and relatively affluent queers, while some of the real sex scenes were injected clumsily into regular scenes in a way that felt purposefully titillating (one moment you'd be watching two women casually walk their dog, and the next they'd be ripping off their J Crew bootcuts and sliding into strap-ons). But at the time the whole thing also felt like a revelation. Here were actual queer women on TV – not as token extras or brief entertainment for the male gaze, but as living, breathing people, with colourful lives, given space to exist in front of a glaring spotlight.

The show garnered more than a cult following. Showtime claimed that *The Real L Word* was its top-performing unscripted show at the time, averaging more than one million viewers during its first two seasons in the US (which is a lot considering how much of the show's popularity continued to grow after it aired). Here in the UK, where it didn't air, young women across the country were tracking down illegal streams with the meticulous perseverance of private detectives, gathering around laptop screens to watch grainy episodes online. I was one of them. My friends and I would spend long weekends binge-watching the three consecutive seasons, passing a blunt across our scratchy uni halls' sofa with hands covered in Papa John's pizza grease before starting the process all over again. By the time I reached graduation, I could recite more quotes from *The Real L Word* than any of the set texts I'd been made to write essays on.

It's hard to tell what made it such gripping television. But it was more than the fact it was messy, off-the-cuff voyeurism in the same vein as, say, *Jersey Shore* or *Geordie Shore*. It was also how it portrayed queer women in a way they hadn't been before. The show wasn't confined to salaciously dredging up cast members' past traumas, or giving them bit parts in a wider, heteronormative narrative (although there were small doses of both). These were communities of women living their regular lives; whether that consisted of juggling a complicated spiderweb of drunken hook-ups, like Whitney in the first season, or having to navigate the gruelling reality of IVF, like long-term couple Kacy and Cori in the second and third.

It's not that anything on the show was particularly unusual or even always meaningful either – to many queer women watching, these were relatable scenes, or at least they were to a certain American demographic. But that was the draw: before then, many of us hadn't seen queer women's lives reflected back at us so openly and casually. 2010 was three years before *Orange Is the New Black*, eight years before *Killing Eve,* nine years before *Gentleman Jack*. It had been less than a decade since we'd first seen two women physically in bed together on a TV series (not even having sex), in the sixth season of *Buffy*. But these were fictional depictions. It was fine to have lesbian and bi characters written into a script, where writers could control how much they were revealing and when they could exit the storyline. But real queer women? Being normal? Being messy and drunk and perving on each other like we see straight people doing all the time? That was unheard of, and therefore *The Real L Word* was a special kind of treasure. It was as if a certain queer language, a private way of being, had been pushed into the public sphere for once – however briefly and absurdly. The first time I watched it, I remember laughing out loud. How ridiculous it was. *How joyous.*

For many though, the joy of watching the show wasn't just about seeing themselves – it was more complicated than that. In a 2017 piece for *VICE*, lesbian author Katie Heaney explained how *The Real L Word* felt like the queer community she'd never experienced in real life. 'I'm greedy,' she wrote. 'I want a lesbian gang. I want a queer community so big and so messily intertwined we fill up a whole bar. I want my own *Real L Word*. But the closest I've been able to get is watching the one on television.' For those who hadn't come out yet, or lived in more isolated or homophobic environments, the show was a portal into what life could be like in a parallel universe; how you could sleep with a different woman each month, fall in love, have a bunch of queer pals to tell you when you're being a dick. You could get married if you wanted to. You could have a stripper party at your house. You could do lesbian mud wrestling in the garden and the sky wouldn't cave in. Real queer people on TV can act as examples – they show that other lives are possible – and *The Real L Word* demonstrated that aplenty. All of this is important in measurable ways: studies have consistently shown that greater queer media representation inspires queer viewers to feel more comfortable in their identities, and therefore more able to come out to themselves and others.

Like most reality shows though, particularly from that era, the story behind the scenes of *The Real L World* wasn't quite so full of light and ease. The queer women on the show were commodities first and foremost, there to lift the veil on the minutiae of their lives to appease starving audiences. If they wanted queer women to be on screen, if they wanted to be part of history, then they'd have to hand over their private lives.

Whitney was twenty-eight when they began filming. She had recently moved to LA from New York, although, unlike a lot of people who do the same thing, harboured no dreams of becoming a television personality. She didn't actually know what she was going to do other than continue working as a special-effects make-up artist when she could and going with the flow when she couldn't, just like she always had done.

When a friend of hers got a casting call for an unscripted queer reality show, Whitney agreed to come along for support and audition too. As these things often play out, her friend didn't get through, but she did. The producers were drawn to Whitney's natural magnetism, her immediate ease in front of a camera and the way she didn't seem to edit her behaviour for a perceived audience. Her love life was already complicated, they just needed to stick a camera there to record it all. Most of the drama seems to revolve around her – especially in the first season – and she's the only key character to have been cast for all three seasons. She had no qualms about being herself on screen, and that included letting them film the occasional sex scene. The producers must have thought they'd stumbled across a goldmine.

Now thirty-seven and still living in LA, Whitney says the show was fun for a while, but it was also incredibly invasive. She hadn't realised how much they would want from her, how much they would take. 'Being Showtime, there was nothing that was off-limits in terms of content. They could film me in the bedroom, in the bathroom, anything – and they did,' she remembers. 'They would basically show up at about eight in the morning, wait for me to wake up, and then they were with me until I went to sleep.'

She describes hiding around her own house, trying to dodge the ever-present lens. 'I would try to get around the cameras, so they would literally stick people outside my house or in my laundry room because they thought I wasn't being truthful about going to bed a couple of times, which was true. It was crazy. There were times when I tried to put my foot down, because there were microphones left in my bedroom, things like that. I didn't know what I was getting myself into.'

As soon as that first episode aired, Whitney immediately began getting recognised. 'I remember going to the gym and I literally felt this silent wave coming towards me gradually,' she recalls. Mainly though, she was a well-known face among queer women, and little known elsewhere. Say her name and most straight people won't know who you're on about. But lesbian and bi women would flock to her. It's often like this with LGBTQ people, especially women: we have our own stars and idols, invisible or simply uninteresting to external communities. 'Whenever Pride would take place, I could not walk around freely,' Whitney says. 'I was a red flag. Especially because I had a very distinct look, so I stuck out like a sore thumb.'

Whitney might have felt constantly dogged by the cameras, but to her it was a sacrifice that needed to be made in order to get real queer women on screen. 'I'll be honest in saying that I could feel the weight of the situation, and the energy behind it – especially with *The L Word* leaving television. There was this void where people wanted to see representation of themselves,' she speaks slowly, carefully, as if mulling it over. 'But also, I was from New York and living in Los Angeles. I was in these incredibly liberal pockets of the country. So it wasn't until I started travelling around the world and putting on events and interacting with people in small-town USA that I started really seeing the impact the show had on people. I have a high level of gratitude for being able to make any type of impact on that level.'

Whitney wasn't the only one who traded her innermost privacy on *The Real L Word* for what was perceived as a greater good. Kacy and Cori Boccumini, married at the time, appear in the second and third series. They're a wholesome, solid unit – the kind of lesbians that even the most conservative pockets of middle America might be able to get their heads around – and desperately want to start a family. You see the whole unflinching process play out on screen: the difficulty in finding sperm donors, the clinical nature of IVF, how tough it can be to get pregnant. And then, heartbreakingly, you watch as Cori finally becomes pregnant before losing their baby girl at five months gestation. Those later episodes are particularly painful to watch: they cry, holding each other, and you feel as though you're intruding on somebody's rawest, most intimate grief. 'I feel like we shouldn't be here,' I remember an ex commenting when we watched those episodes. But it was also the first time we'd seen the real practicalities behind two women starting a family. It sounds naive, but before then I'd assumed having kids wasn't really an option for most people like me.

Kacy says they largely knew what they were getting into. It was a trade-off they were prepared to make. 'We got asked a bunch of questions like, "Would we inseminate on camera?" How detailed and how intimate into the process of making the baby would we allow them to be?' she remembers. 'You know the episode where Romi and Whitney have sex? Imagine that, but then they make a baby. They didn't directly say that, but that was the picture they were starting to paint for us. And I was like, "Okay, okay I get what you want. I'll think about it".' They genuinely didn't think they'd make the final cut, she says, so what was there to lose?

Mainly, though, there was this overarching feeling of wanting to give something back, to create the visibility that had been so lacking when they were kids. Kacy presents as butch, with cropped hair and men's jeans and caps and waistcoats. In the 2000s, when femme lipstick lesbians were having a sort of moment thanks to shows like *The L Word* and bi characters like Alex Kelly on *The OC*, butches were often relegated to the sidelines. 'I'm not "Shane" butch. I'm a curvy, full-figured woman who shoves D breasts into a men's button-down shirt, puts on a tie and goes to work. I'm a butch woman. I'd never seen that on TV. I remember thinking to myself, "If I can show other girls like me that it is possible to have a wife, a family and be happy then this is worth it".'

Kacy and Cori were also one of 18,000 same-sex couples who were legally married in a country that had recently outlawed it. To explain: in 2008, California Supreme Court announced that it would legally recognise gay marriage. One year later, due to a huge backlash from religious and conservative organisations across the US, that law was overturned. But the marriages that occurred within that time frame were still technically legal, including Kacy and Cori's. During the filming of *The Real L Word*, then, the urgency surrounding gay rights felt particularly heightened. Their privilege as a married couple was one they took seriously. 'It did colour our situation very differently,' Kacy says. 'We felt a lot of responsibility to be a really good solid married couple. To show that it was worth it, to fight for marriage equality.'

Their contribution wasn't an empty one. For a lot of viewers, Kacy and Cori showed that a more conventional lifestyle was possible, if that was what you wanted. You could be a butch lesbian and still have kids and marriage like your parents did; it didn't have to be an 'us versus them' between gays and their heteronormative or conservative families. 'So many women reached out to me and were like, "Thank you so much, because I was able to show my mum *The L Real Word*, and I look like you and they could see that you had a beautiful partner and this loving marriage and great relationship and it was easier on my

mum to accept me as gay because you were a shining example".
And the weight of that and knowing how different I would be if
I'd had the same made it all worth it.'

By June 2015, the US Supreme Court had struck down all state
bans on same-sex marriage, legalising it in all fifty states. Whitney
says that in the years since, she's noticed a tangible shift in the way
lesbian and bi people are portrayed on television. It's not that she
thinks there are more or fewer queer characters, per se, but that
their orientation isn't their central personality trait, even on reality
shows. There's more nuance and fluidity, perhaps – it's become less
of a big deal. 'It started shifting,' she says. '[Your sexuality] became
a secondary thing, a breakdown of a character. And though that
seems small, it's actually huge. Because you weren't leading with
this thing that defines you, it was just a part of your life. And I
think that really shifted the tone.'

While this fluidity is appreciated, Kacy thinks we've still got a
long way to go when it comes to lesbians on screen specifically.
'The representations that I see on television . . . I don't feel truly
represent what "being a lesbian" is. What I think of as being a
lesbian is someone who isn't burdened or bothered by the presence of what a man might think. Men are taken out of that
conversation in terms of sexuality. They just don't factor into
anything that we do. How we look. How we speak. The volume
of our voice. The way in which we show or don't show our
bodies. It's free and void of that gaze. And I don't think anybody's
really got that right yet.'

§

To truly understand the effect that shows like *The Real L Word*
had, we need to first rewind a little. If you asked me to recall the
first time I saw a queer woman on television – real or fictional – it

would take a while to pinpoint. It could have been Ellen DeGeneres, who has been a staple on mainstream television for well over three decades, but who also represents a very rich, white American version of what a lesbian looks like. It could have been Susan and Carol on the sitcom *Friends*, who are presented as happy and content, but whose relationship is also the butt of a long-standing joke (Ross can't get over the shock of his ex-wife leaving him for another woman; how embarrassing!) Or maybe it was that *Sex and the City* episode in which Samantha realises she likes sleeping with women too, and temporarily describes herself as a lesbian. Although, that soon changes once she realises that queer women might give phenomenal head, but once they've ensnared you with their tongue all they want to do is have bubble baths and chat about their feelings all day (God forbid Samantha explore her queerness beyond one 'crazy' lesbian relationship – another stereotype we'll come back to in this book).

Before the 2010s, representations of queer women on television both here in the UK and overseas were rare and relatively two-dimensional. Actual queer women in the public eye were often white, middle class, cisgender, politically 'respectable' and therefore considered palatable for a specific and narrow mainstream audience (Ellen DeGeneres, Rosie O'Donnell, Cynthia Nixon). Those who were fictional often appeared as some weird sub-plot that either resulted in the queer character realising their sexuality was just a phase (as with Samantha in *Sex and the City*), experiencing just one brief and unexpected lesbian kiss (called 'perfect sweeps stunts' in 2005 by the TV critic Virginia Heffernan, due to the fact they appeased queers and caused controversy without ever fully committing) or else dying an untimely and violent death (a trope so common it's been dubbed 'Dead Lesbian Syndrome' on the internet). In fact, when online LGBTQ magazine *Autostraddle* examined 1,779 scripted American television series from 1976 to

2016, just 11 per cent of them featured lesbian or bisexual women. Among those characters, 35 per cent ended up dead, with only 16 per cent provided with some sort of happy ending. Over the years, this had a weird effect on the queer viewing experience. Every time a lesbian or bi character popped up in a soap or TV drama, you'd half expect a hammer to fly out of a nearby bush and randomly bludgeon her on the head.

It's hard to know why Dead Lesbian Syndrome became such a long-standing trope, but people have their own theories. Lesbian and bi characters are considered more disposable than their straight counterparts, perhaps, or are being subconsciously punished for their imagined sins. Maybe straight writers are used to viewing lesbian and bi women through the lens of tragedy or trauma and are unable to envision a narrative outside of that. I personally think that straight or male writers sometimes simply don't know what to do with their queer women characters in the long term. It's easier to have them unexpectedly flattened by a passing truck than to have to keep writing about their mysterious lives, which probably involve scissoring and complicated types of milk and words like 'futch'.

Another theory I've encountered time and time again is that straight or male writers assume that stories about queer women simply don't interest anybody other than queer women. They're too 'niche'. There aren't enough queer women in the world to watch them and straight people only like watching shows about other straight people or gay men at a push, otherwise they'll turn the TV off (What could two women possibly be getting up to when men aren't around?! Brushing each other's hair?).

But this is a flimsy concept that bears no connection to reality. There are millions of queer women hiding in coffee shops and libraries, and straight people, just like us, can generally put themselves in another's shoes (wild, I know). As such, the few queer shows that managed to get it 'right' throughout the 2000s tended to garner diehard fanbases. The rare shows that centred lesbian and bi women became overnight cult sensations, while queer narratives enjoyed an immediate word-of-mouth fame quite unlike that of straight stories of a similar ilk.

In the UK, this is exactly how it played out with *Sugar Rush*, a 2005 Channel 4 drama based on the Julie Burchill novel of the same name. For a lot of queer women in their twenties and thirties, *Sugar Rush* will have been their first proper encounter with lesbian or bi narratives on television (minus someone like Sonia on *EastEnders* randomly snogging a neighbour.) It arrived just a year after *The L Word* in the US. Very quickly, the two seasons of *Sugar Rush* became staple viewing for queer girls across the country.

Based in Brighton, the show follows fifteen-year-old Kim, who harbours a secret crush on her lip-glossed, spaghetti-strapped, denim-skirted and vocally hetero best mate Sugar. But the relatable queer storyline isn't the show's only draw: it's also about drinking, drugs, complicated family dynamics and growing up in a small British town while sexually confused and bored out of your mind (in other words: relatable to a lot of British teens, not just lesbians and bi girls). Plus, it arrived a year before the UK drama series *Skins*, which normalised many of those subjects. In more ways than one it was a primer for what young people wanted, all set to a mid-2000s soundtrack of Goldfrapp, Basement Jaxx, Bloc Party and Sugababes.

I don't fully remember how I got hold of *Sugar Rush* back then, pre-internet-streaming – maybe a DVD from the local library? A pink plastic thing, covered in bubbly font – but I remember the feeling it gave me, what it still reminds me of. The show distils the obsessive horniness of being a teenager combined with the confusion of being a queer one; the adolescent bliss of being in the messy, perfumed bedroom of a girl you fancy. Getting dizzy on Fanta and Glen's vodka while bunking off school. Cigarette smoke and warm, darting tongues on the drizzly seafront. *Sugar Rush* isn't just about the weird difficulties of being a closeted lesbian in love with your straight best mate – it's about the twisted pleasure of it. How all of these things can disorientate and excite you, even when you feel as though you're multiple people arguing with each other internally. And how, in some ways, unrequited love can act as a cornerstone of queer teen sexuality, giving you space to explore your queerness safely and privately before jumping into the real thing.

For me, it was the first time I'd come across a queer experience that semi-mirrored my own. Kim wrestles with her gayness, occasionally imagines it isn't there, spends a lot of time being homophobic to herself while also desperate for some action, drooling over Sugar every time she glances in her direction. For those struggling to get to grips with their sexuality, Kim's confused, horny, contradictory inner thoughts (which appear as spoken narration throughout) can feel like listening in on the shit that used to swim around your own head. 'She's not gay,' Kim thinks aloud about Sugar in the first ten minutes of the pilot. 'And I don't want to be.' Crucially though, her horniness overrides her internalised homophobia. Kim never dives back into the closet. She finds a girlfriend. Moves in with her. Leans into her queerness in a way that made teenage me think, 'Oh this isn't such a big deal after all, is it?'

I'm not the only person for whom *Sugar Rush* was an important formative viewing experience. During its short time on air, the show blew up massively, winning an Emmy Award in 2006 followed by a BAFTA nomination in 2007. When I do a quick shout-out online asking queer women what *Sugar Rush* meant to them as closeted teens, my inbox fills up with replies from

Manchester, Birmingham, Norwich, small towns from around the UK. 'It was everythingggg,' types one woman in her mid-twenties. 'That show literally changed my life,' types another. 'Pretty monumental,' types another, 'I moved to Brighton. Sat on the seafront where they filmed it. Still can't believe it got cancelled.' Teddy Edwardes, who now runs a queer club night in London called LICK, tells me that watching *Sugar Rush* was the catalyst for her finally realising she was into girls. 'I remember watching it for the first time and being like . . . Wow, I'm *gay* gay.'

More than just enjoying *Sugar Rush*, from chatting to these fans I sense that there's a unifying nature central to the enjoyment; it's almost an in-joke, a virtual adolescence we shared together. Fandom in general tends to work like that: you consume something in private, it speaks to you personally, and then you connect with others over that private experience. But queer fandom goes one step further. If you're familiar with the specific feeling that comes with queer isolation, as if you're the only person who feels a certain way, then the joint love of a piece of pop culture can be really healing; it fills you up. And this is the case whether we're chatting about queer girls in the 1990s passing around homemade zines about Team Dresch, millennials reminiscing over *Sugar Rush* or young queer teens today creating *Euphoria* meme accounts.

Olivia Hallinan, the actress who played Kim, says she still receives gushing letters from queer women today about how the show changed their lives. Olivia has never been anything like Kim. At thirty-five she now has a husband and children and dogs and likes walks through nature and yoga in the sunshine. But people still think of Olivia as the confused fifteen-year-old lesbian from Brighton who smokes fags and stares broodily out over the pier. 'It spoke to people who had maybe gone through a hard time accepting themselves,' she tells me. 'I have to be like, "It wasn't me! It was my character! But I'll take it." I have people come up to me and cry, saying, "You don't understand how much *Sugar Rush* helped me come out", and I'm like, "Wow, that's amazing". Maybe people didn't have anything they could relate to. And then suddenly, I guess they did.'

Like Whitney and Kacy, there's pride in Olivia's voice when she speaks about how *Sugar Rush* paved the way for queer characters on TV. She said she was only twenty-one when she accepted the role and had never heard of the book it was based on. She wasn't even sure she wanted to do it at first because the 'lesbian schoolgirl' storyline sounded fetishistic (itself an indicator of how queer women had been represented on screen beforehand). But it was the opposite. And in the years since, Olivia has seen the impact the show has had on culture in a much wider sense. 'I think it definitely opened doors in terms of showing same-sex relationships. There hadn't been much before then – maybe *Queer as Folk*? But none with girls,' she says. 'After that, it was okay to show that on screen. I don't know why it was such a taboo subject before. *Sugar Rush* dared to go where TV *should* go. From then, you saw it more frequently.'

Olivia's right. In the years since *Sugar Rush* aired, television that centralises queer women and therefore caters to a queer women audience has gradually become a lot more common. Not just for cisgender white people either, but for trans people and people of colour too (although it's worth pointing out here that non-binary stories in particular are still painfully rare on TV screens). That said, it took some time and there's still a long way to go. As Maya Salam points out in a piece for the *New York Times*, late 2000s shows like *The L Word* laid some important groundwork, but it wasn't until after it went off the air in 2009 that more concrete progress and compelling representations started to flourish – including among characters of colour. Such women became integral on highly popular shows like *House* (2004–2012), *Grey's Anatomy* (2005–present), *Glee* (2009–2015), *Pretty Little Liars* (2010–2017) and *How to Get Away with Murder* (2014–2020).

Shows such as *The L Word, The Real L Word,* and *Sugar Rush* here in the UK can be viewed as lines in the sand. In the past half-decade, major conglomerates like Netflix, HBO and Amazon Prime have given us a whole host of shiny, properly budgeted shows relating to queer characters: *Orange Is the New Black, Transparent, Euphoria, Trinkets, I Am Not Okay With This.* These are shows that centre the queer experience in a way that often feels incidental, non-sensationalist and a far cry from the Susan-and-Carol side plots of yesteryear. In 2019, we also saw a reboot of *The L Word: The L Word: Generation Q* (the 'Q' standing for 'queer'), with a much more diverse crowd alongside the original cast. *Generation Q*, while still upholding its naff and ridiculous writing, was inclusive without feeding into the same old queer tropes historically seen on mainstream television. 'There are no coming-out stories here, no tortured hand-wringing over identity, just characters who are all queer in some way, living big, messy lives,' wrote Rebecca Nicholson in a *Guardian* review. How far we seem to have come.

The rise of queer characters on screen isn't just conjecture. According to GLAAD's annual TV diversity report, LGBTQ representation on American television hit a record high in 2018, with 8.8 per cent out of 857 series regulars on broadcast television openly identifying on the gay, trans or queer spectrum, with 50 per cent of them being people of colour. Similar data doesn't currently exist for the UK, but the ripple effect can be felt way beyond America's borders. In the last couple of years alone, we've had BBC dramas *Gentleman Jack* and *Killing Eve* and

Channel 4 comedies *The Bisexual* and *Feel Good*, all of which star complicated, sexual and confident queer women. These are popular, critically lauded shows on mainstream channels. The old notion that the only people interested in the lives of queers are queers themselves seems to be stripping away, ever so slowly. These aren't just shows watched by lesbians and bi women. They're watched by their fifty-something-year-old hetero parents too. They're watched by their straight mates' boyfriends.

All of this is an important start. For a lot of people I spoke to for this book, when they were teenagers, queer TV was a rare and secret treat. They described covertly downloading episodes of 2002 drama *Tipping the Velvet* via LimeWire, or else waiting until their parents were out of the house before watching *The L Word* with the volume turned down, finger poised over the pause button just in case someone unexpectedly came home. Shauna told me how she had a tiny pink TV at the bottom of her bed as a teenager with an in-built DVD player ('There's probably a metaphor in there somewhere. Something about a tiny pink object being the portal to my queerdom'). After her mum had turned off the lights and gone to sleep, she'd stay up late watching shows like *Sugar Rush* or the third and fourth series of *Skins*, the ones with the lesbians.

In some ways, I've always thought that there is a delicious joy in discovering and exploring your sexuality alone and in secret like this. There's a purity to the way in which queerness becomes a conversation with yourself about truth and authenticity and desire, a slow and subconscious one, which trickles under the surface of your skin and only starts to bloom once you see two women lock lips in a soap one night or a teenager on TV admitting they want to stare at their best mate's tits. 'That feels a bit like me,' you think quietly, the idea stirring something imperceptible in your chest, the subconscious internal conversation rising ever so slightly closer to the surface. The more you watch, the closer that conversation springs into being, until it's screaming at you.

But we also shouldn't have to treat queer culture as if we are secretly addicted to an illicit drug. I can't imagine it's particularly healthy for anybody's sense of self having to keep one part of yourself guiltily hidden away, fragmenting your identity. Any instance in which queerness is normalised on television helps meld these fragments together. The more queer characters we see on TV, the less we feel as though there are parts of ourselves that should remain hidden, buried like unsavoury perversions. 'If I hadn't got so into *Sugar Rush* I reckon it would have taken me a lot longer to realise I was gay,' one lesbian tells me. 'Then once that realisation hits you, the rest of your life kind of clicks into place.'

What we see on TV ripples through every corner of society too. While films and songs and books are important platforms when it comes to queer narratives, television is a lot more pervasive, it's all-encompassing, consumed by all generations in the most pedestrian of settings. It's that normal, quotidian thing that lives in your lounge and that your mum watches *The Voice* on. In a 2015 study by the Broadcast Education Association it was found that after viewing many hours of programming featuring gay characters, 'a positive relationship existed between viewing gay characters on television and endorsement of gay equality' among straight participants. What's more, this correlation was stronger for straight people who didn't have any gay mates. Seeing queer characters on TV, then, doesn't just make queer people feel more comfortable in their own skin. Representation actively contributes to a more equal and fair society. Which can only be a good thing, right?

Mainly though, watching TV that only features straight people is really boring, regardless of where you land on the sexuality scale.

There isn't only one type of person in the world, so why should there be only one type of person on our screens? It's like saying you only like eating sausages, and therefore you only want to be around other people who eat sausages and go to restaurants with a strictly sausage-only menu. Mix it up a bit, why don't you. We don't all like eating sausages. Some of us prefer oysters.

Part Two: Film

A few years back I found myself at a relative's house, steadily making my way through a packet of custard creams on the sofa with some family friends and speaking about the film *Carol*. I had loved it, I said, making vague references to the immaculate 1950s outfits and intense orchestral score. But what I truly loved about that film had more to do with the fact that it was a realistic romance between two women (one of whom is played by Cate Blanchett, who I happen to have a massive crush on). Not only that, but neither of them had been violently murdered or 'decided' to become straight at the end, and the way their relationship had unfolded on screen was more relatable, and engaging, than anything else I'd seen at the cinema in recent memory.

One of my family friends said they'd also enjoyed the film for a variety of reasons. 'I don't mean this to be offensive . . .' she then said, in that way that often preludes something offensive. I bit down on another custard cream. 'But before watching *Carol*, I just didn't realise two women could really, really *fancy* each other like that, you know? I guess I just always thought queer women . . . secretly wanted to be straight.'

Her comment stuck with me for a long time. Not because I found it insulting – she didn't mean it in a venomous way – but because it revealed some sort of fundamental truth, one that I'd not fully grasped beforehand, and still couldn't, like the root of an unknown plant obscured by soil. And for years I found myself returning to her words, rolling them around in my mind and wondering if this was a misconception shared by anyone else – and if so, why? What was at the centre of what she was saying?

Did other people think the same thing? Was this family friend simply saying out loud what a lot of straight people would never admit to? Where had her thoughts sprung from? But also, what was it about *Carol* in particular that had altered this person's reality, rather than any other piece of art involving queerness? Before *Carol*, she assumed queer women were begrudgingly half-pretending to fancy each other, that they didn't fully feel it. And after *Carol* she realised that we weren't. And if that was the case, what does that say about the power of films in general, or the lack of films like *Carol* in the public eye beforehand?

Once those questions unfolded themselves, more questions sprang in their place, and I began to peer closely at my own conceptions. I thought about men for a moment, with their hairy solidness and musky chests and heavy sleeping bodies. Why, before *Carol*, didn't my family friend understand that desire could exist between two women, while I (and other lesbians, I presume) understood that desire could exist between a man and a woman, or two men, or other genders? I suppose I didn't understand it always, intimately, but I believed it intrinsically because I had seen it everywhere – in real life and pop culture from the moment I'd been born – and therefore assumed it to be true.

In other words, I knew that I might want certain people, and others might want other people, and while the objects of desire might differ among us, at different times in our lives even, the *desire itself* was essentially the same. And that, it seems, is a realisation that my family friend only came to after watching *Carol*.

§

Carol arrived in 2015, which, for general context, was the same year same-sex marriage was legalised federally across America by Barack Obama, Caitlyn Jenner came out as trans on the cover of *Vanity Fair* and Donald Trump began to inch ever closer to becoming America's president – so, a mixed bag. *Carol* was director Todd Haynes's sixth full-length feature film and it was based on the cult Patricia Highsmith novel *The Price of Salt*, which had first been published from 1952 up until the mid-nineties under a pseudonym (she'd called herself 'Claire Morgan' back then). Most significantly though, *The Price of Salt* was known and celebrated for being the first piece of lesbian fiction with a happy ending.

Carol wasn't the first lesbian film to have a happy ending by any stretch of the imagination – but it was definitely one of the most widely known and advertised (perhaps unsurprising for an American blockbuster with two cis, white, femme A-lister leads. Cheryl Dunye's 1996 New Queer Cinema classic *The Watermelon Woman*, for instance – the first feature film by and about a Black lesbian – could also be seen as having a 'happy' ending, if we are to measure such a thing in terms of self-actualisation rather than romance). Even so, *Carol* had an extremely difficult time getting funded and endured a number of struggles and setbacks before becoming a reality. When it was first adapted into a film script back in 1997 (yep, nearly two decades before it was actually released) hardly anybody wanted to touch it. In fact, it didn't lift off the ground properly until the introduction of Cate Blanchett in 2012, and it took until 2013 for Haynes to come on board and for the film to go into pre-production.

It would be easy to assume that investors weren't interested in *Carol* because it's a film about lesbians, and who is interested in a couple of lesbians brushing hands and giving each other loaded glances other than lesbians themselves, unless it's porn and/or a murder? But the truth is maybe even more depressing: according to those who worked on *Carol*, the initial lack of support was – put simply – because it's a film starring women. *Brokeback Mountain* might have received accolades a decade prior, but swap the two lead men for women and the funding dries up. 'Cate and Rooney [Mara] are in every single frame,' Haynes shrugged to the *Guardian* in response to this very subject. 'It has no lead men.'

Screenwriter Phyllis Nagy, a close friend of Highsmith's who went on to write the *Carol* screenplay two years after her death in 1995, has echoed a similar sentiment to Haynes. 'My feeling, having talked to and tried to put it together with so many people over the years, is not so much it being gay women; it's about it being women,' she told the *Guardian* in 2015. 'In film-financing terms, that's very tricky. It's very sad that I have to say this. But even *Thelma & Louise* was a generation ago. The 1930s and 40s were nothing but celebrations of fantastically complex female leads. We've lost that.'

Later, in that same interview, Nagy makes an interesting point about the queer women she'd encountered in recent films, prior to *Carol*. She said she'd noticed a swing back to 'vampy' queer characters on screen, 'like Susan Sarandon and Catherine Deneuve à la *The Hunger*. You turn on the TV and there's hot young dykes or bisexuals.' But gay and bi women with multi-layered narratives on the big screen? That was hugely lacking in the film world. She wondered whether the strongest argument for how stories like *Carol* can succeed, and do have broad audiences, would perhaps be *Carol* itself. 'If this movie does well, maybe three other movies like it can be made,' she told the interviewer. 'And then if those movies do well . . .'

Essentially, if *Carol* made money, maybe it would open doors for a less salacious, campy version of female queerness (Abdellatif Kechiche's 2013 French romance *Blue is the Warmest Colour* came close, but the graphic sex scenes and typically melancholy ending made it more of an acquired taste than a mainstream game-changer. Plus, both lead actresses later spoke out about the male director's poor treatment of them, specifically with regard to filming the sex scenes, which rightly tainted the viewing experience). In other words, maybe lesbian and bi films didn't have to be niche indie favourites, or rife with trauma and death. Maybe they could be romantic blockbusters, too. The kind of film your nan might watch on a Sunday night with a cup of tea and plate of Bourbons. Or a love story that both straight and queer kids might fantasise about, the way I used to play and replay old VHS tapes of *Titanic*, crying privately and dramatically whenever the panpipes started and the camera zoomed in on Rose's pale icy face.

Nagy needn't have worried. *Carol* did well – astonishingly well – in comparison to expectations. As of 2018, it had made a worldwide total of around $43 million against a $11.8 million budget. During awards season, the film received six Oscar nominations, including Best Actress for Cate Blanchett and co-star Rooney Mara, as well as five Golden Globe Award nominations, including Best Motion Picture. A year after its release, the British Film Institute named *Carol* the best LGBTQ film of all time, according to over one hundred film experts in a poll encompassing more than eighty years of cinema. Finally, money had been pumped into a love story with lesbian leads and had been given the same treatment as a big hetero blockbuster.

The result was a sumptuous, velveteen romance, full of curling cigarette smoke and metaphorical gloves and intoxicating silences. 'What a strange girl you are . . .' Carol says in the film to her soon-to-be lover Therese, played by Mara, her deep voice lilting, clouded eyes drifting into her martini, '. . . flung out of space.' It's a line you want to breathe in and climb inside; real life magnified and given room to be tasted properly. Watching it back now, it's no wonder my family friend suddenly believed wholeheartedly in the mechanics of queer love. It's just interesting that this is all it took: one major film.

§

Today, the indicator of a successful film isn't necessarily how many critics give it five stars or laud it as a 'triumph' – although, with *Carol*, there were many. It isn't even how many awards and accolades the film racks up, or indeed how much money it makes at the box office during opening weekend – again, *Carol* did standardly well in those departments for a film of its size. Instead, it's got a lot more to do with how it exists on the internet. Specifically fandom, and how the collective love of a piece of pop culture can bloom and multiply and flourish online, inhabiting a life of its own far beyond the film's initial release cycle.

This is what happened with *Carol*, which is a strange thing to happen to a 1950s-based melodrama with hardly any dialogue – especially one with a budget and profile that doesn't even closely compare to, say, the Twilight franchise or any of the Marvel films, both of which have their own hardcore fanbases. But these are queer women we're talking about, and the *Carol* disciples came out in full force. Seemingly overnight, fan art Tumblrs, Facebook groups, Twitter accounts, lengthy subreddit threads and painstakingly put-together YouTube edits dedicated to the film began to crop up everywhere.

GIFs were shared and in-jokes abounded. One Tumblr user posted on 11 December 2015 about a scene they'd encountered at the cinema earlier that year: 'I really don't know what crowd I expected to be in the theatre for *Carol* at 1:20 in the afternoon on a Friday, but it was probably 85 per cent old het couples, and halfway through the movie this old lady in front of me turned to the old dude next to her and just said "Harold, they're lesbians".'

Quickly, 'Harold they're lesbians' became a widely shared meme among the *Carol* fandom and beyond, with the word 'Harold' becoming a catch-all internet phrase for anything lesbian-related. 'I want a shirt that just says "HAROLD",' wrote one Tumblr user. 'It will be my secret mating call. My family would never know the significance, but the ladygays would and that's all that matters.'

Often the hype around a film peaks and then plateaus. But two years later, and the fanatic momentum behind *Carol* still hadn't died down. Even Cate Blanchett, who has appeared in *The Lord of the Rings* for God's sake, noted that this was unusual. 'I've been stopped in the supermarket by more people about *Carol* than I have with any other film,' she told *Variety*. 'If a film doesn't necessarily linger at the box office, that doesn't mean it won't have a reach. There are so many platforms for people to encounter films now that our sense of a film's success really needs to be a lot more elastic.'

Allison Tate, an LA-based writer and director, noticed how obsessed everyone still was with *Carol* and decided to create a short comedy about it called *Carol Support Group*. In the eight-minute clip, which you can still find online, various *Carol* addicts come together to share their stories in a Narcotics

Anonymous-style group circle. One is wearing a Christmas hat (like Therese at the beginning of the film). Another is clutching a plastic doll in reference to the toy department Therese works in. Everyone is in 1950s-style outfits, repeatedly throwing out well-known lines from *Carol* ('A strange girl . . . flung out of space.')

Eventually the group descends into chaos after a woman called Blanche (a play on 'Blanchett') seduces them all while wearing a fox fur jacket and *Carol*-style curled hair. It's quite a funny watch. Not necessarily because of the script, but because it overtly acknowledges the strange fervour behind the film and how absurd and self-aware and joyful the whole thing feels.

'When the trailer dropped, I watched it every day. It became my morning ritual,' Allison tells me over the phone from her home in Silverlake, LA. Hearing her speak about *Carol* sounds a bit like hearing someone gush about when they first met their long-time lover: the moments leading up to it, the moments after, the sweaty palms, the intoxicating endorphins, how their life changed. I'd find her reaction almost outlandish if I, too, weren't so obsessed with *Carol*. But I am, so I get it.

'I will never forget the first time I saw that ending shot . . . *whew!*' she continues, speaking about the scene right at the end, when Therese walks into a restaurant to meet Carol, and the two look at each other like they want to wear each other's skin, forever. The final shot is from Therese's perspective. Carol is gazing at her intently, blue eyes sparkling. You want to dive inside them and go for a swim. 'It hit me like nothing else has ever hit me before. It's like Carol is looking right at you, through your soul and entire being,' Allison says, laughing but also deadly serious. 'The only way I can describe it is a look of unconditional love. That's what I felt it was. I felt like I could do anything in that moment. I truly felt like she would always be there for me. I could come back to her anytime; I could share my childlike excitement, my trials, my pitfalls. I felt like I could achieve anything I wanted to achieve.'

Allison was working as a producer at LGBTQ magazine *The Advocate* when she put *Carol Support Group* together. She tells me the film became something to focus on, something in which she could channel her *Carol* addiction in a healthy, 'productive way'. But it also felt like it was a gift for all the lesbian and bi women who were just as obsessed as she was. 'People from all over the world reached out to me afterwards,' she says. 'People said it was like seeing their own inner monologue, that they felt seen, that it was a gift to the fandom. I felt like I was a member of that group, and I saw the need, and was able to put my skills and talents into something and give back.'

Allison sees *Carol* as a watershed moment. Not just because it's a film about lesbians with a happy ending, but because it's what she calls a 'prestige' film. It's about gay women, sure, but it's also cinematically beautiful, properly budgeted and stars critically lauded A-listers alongside a director known for his craft. This combination, Allison says, was the key that cracked the code.

'I don't think up until that point we had a film as finely crafted *and* about queer women,' she explains. 'We'd been living on scraps for so long . . . I mean, I don't want to diminish the creations that came out before. But it does feel like that. Especially if you're someone who loves art films, savours them – but you don't *feel* yourself in those things. You're going to feel like you're missing out. And that's just how queer people move through the world. Or that's how I've felt. So to get that kind of attention made me feel like, "Wow, I am worth it". Queer people do deserve this type of love poured into their stories. We've never had that much love and attention in a film.'

A few weeks later, Allison emails me out of the blue. She says she's been thinking a lot about our conversation on the phone, about why *Carol* was a turning point and why it got people so hooked. 'It's almost an impossible question to answer because it's like asking what makes you fall in love,' she says. 'But another factor that I think made people fall in love with it is the way that queer people communicate, and communicated during those times, was so marvellously captured. The looks of a thousand longings, the touches that spark fire, all the non-verbal communication that is signature to many queer experiences was the main language of the film.

'I certainly felt like I was seeing a new film language, one that I immediately understood in my bones, and in my subconscious,' she adds. 'I might not have seen it before, but once I did, I knew I was fluent.'

Dr Clara Bradbury-Rance, lecturer and author of the book *Lesbian Cinema After Queer Theory*, echoes a lot of what Allison is saying. *Carol* isn't just beloved by queer women because it's a lesbian love story, she says, but because it embodies the subtle, erotic language of queerness. You know when you make intense eye contact with an 'are they or aren't they a lesbian' that goes on a bit too long? When you try to give off your own queer energy without having to say it? *Carol* takes that secret non-verbal language and bottles it. 'What I think is really extraordinary about *Carol* – which is the reason that I love it – is that it's a lot queerer than all that. It's not just simply a love story,' she explains over cocktails one evening. 'It's a film which is defined by unreturned looks and fleeting touches and gloves . . . and gloves!'

That, says Bradbury-Rance, is what makes *Carol* particularly delicious. It's not just a film about thirst, it's about *queer thirst* and the sexy, almost imperceptible language that sits right at the heart of it.

§

As with all long-lasting obsessions, the fervour around *Carol* eventually evolved into something else. At some point it became less about *Carol* the film specifically, and more broadly about Cate Blanchett, and the idea that she could, in a perfect parallel universe, be gay. This wasn't quite a 'Cate Blanchett is secretly a lesbian and her husband is a beard' thing, in the same vein as, say, the earnest and long-standing theories surrounding the sexuality of Taylor Swift or Kendall Jenner. Rather, it was more of an in-joke/collective fantasy/queer -longing manifested. As if queer women so desperately wanted Cate Blanchett to be queer that we could somehow wish it into being. If enough people could uphold that fantasy, the fantasy might come alive.

A quick scroll through Instagram reveals hundreds of accounts dedicated to Cate Blanchett, nearly all of which are run by young lesbian and bi people. Cate Blanchett in tailored suits. Cate Blanchett with razor-sharp cheekbones. Cate Blanchett with her arm draped around other actresses like they're lovers. Accounts like @dykeblanchett, which has around 35,000 followers, exist solely to meld the worlds of Blanchett and lesbianism together via memes. 'Soft butch Cate Blanchett could cut me with her cheekbones and I would still say thank you in nine different languages,' reads one caption beneath a still of Cate with a shaved head from the 2002 film *Heaven*. 'Brunette Cate Blanchett in *Coffee and Cigarettes* (2003) is the straight girl you're into who you know is going to break your heart but you go along with it anyways,' reads another beneath a monochrome image of the actress, cigarette hanging loosely between two fingers. The comments are crammed with heart-eye faces and fire and beads-of-sweat emojis. 'Honestly ur account makes me forget that Cate Blanchett isn't a full-blown lesbian . . .' writes one follower beneath a picture of Cate and Nicole Kidman looking like the quintessential butch–femme couple.

What strikes me most about these Cate Blanchett stan accounts isn't necessarily the fact that thousands of lesbians and bi kids are coming together to worship at the altar of a fifty-one-year-old actress with a bone structure carved by Aphrodite herself. The mechanics of fandom, and queer women's predilection for middle-aged women in blazers, are both timeless and unsurprising (see: Gillian Anderson, Meryl Streep in *The Devil Wears Prada*, literally any woman who could have been your childhood best friend's mum who was also a power bitch lawyer with amazing tits). It's more that these accounts double up as safe spaces for queer kids to be unrestrained about their sexuality. No one's going to think you're a weirdo for commenting 'Daddy' beneath a picture of Cate Blanchett in thick-rimmed glasses. No one's going to blink twice at you shouting 'BIG TOP ENERGY' or 'SIT ON MY FACE' in all caps with your keyboard. While young people in general have long forged spaces in which to channel their desire for actors/musicians/bands (see: The Beatles, My Chemical Romance, One Direction, Robert Pattinson) queer girls are rarely given the same opportunity to be quite so pervy and open and loud about it. Growing up, we're expected to tack posters of boybands or emo frontmen to our walls, not married women with quiffs and ironed trousers who are probably older than our parents. Within the virtual walls of a Cate Blanchett account, though, queer desire is given room to be expressed publicly.

Most fans tell me that their love of Cate might have begun with *Carol*, but has since outgrown it. Pan Pan, a twenty-three-year-old from Myanmar in Southeast Asia, didn't know who Cate was before *Carol*. 'I didn't fall in love with her at first,' she says. Instead, she found herself constantly returning to the film, watching and rewatching, until she realised that it was Cate who was actually her 'source of joy'. After that, Pan Pan watched all her movies. She set up Cate Blanchett accounts on Twitter and Instagram. Became wrapped up in the fandom. 'I love everything she does; the way she speaks, the way she smiles, each and every part of her face, her body and especially her beautiful soul. I know no one is perfect but even if she does things that I don't like, I still love her. Because she is Cate Blanchett.'

Seventeen-year-old lesbian Ren, from the Midwest in the US, has Cate as her Twitter pic and 'middle-aged actresses' in her bio. She can trace her interest back to watching *Carol* three or four years ago. 'I was immediately star struck by Cate's on-screen presence, look and voice,' she remembers. 'She is breathtakingly gorgeous. I think a lot of it has to do with her entire presence as a person. She is very smart and charismatic, which are two traits everyone wants.' Ren doesn't think it's unusual for queer teens to be stanning a fifty-one-year-old with a husband and kids. 'There are a lot of fandoms like this one.' She shrugs. 'People stan Sarah Paulson, Sandra Bullock and other middle-aged actresses. I think what draws some is perhaps motherly issues, personal attraction and just finding a sense of comfort.'

For twenty-three-year-old non-binary fan Kai, based in LA, *Carol* might have kicked things off but it was Cate's character Lou in the 2018 heist film *Ocean's 8* who really ignited the fuse. Lou never reveals her sexuality, but the choppy hair, aviators and never-ending carousel of loose ties – plus the wry, knowing glances between her and Sandra Bullock's character Debbie – led a lot of viewers to join the queer dots (neither actress has fully confirmed or denied this theory). After *Ocean's 8*, Kai immediately started a Cate Blanchett Twitter account, connected with other fans online, joined group chats full of other queer girls and non-binary people.

Kai has actually seen Cate in the flesh – a rarity among fans who stan actors, who only tend to come out for awards ceremonies and premieres. There's a pinned tweet on their account with them doing the peace sign, their face a mixture of nervous joy and disbelief, hair waving in the breeze. Cate is in the background in a checked blazer and sunglasses, signing posters, sunlight bouncing off her face. 'Does this count as a selfie?' reads the caption. Kai had gone down to an LA premiere of *The House with a Clock in its Walls* with a few other queer fans, all of them hoping to catch a glimpse of those clear blue eyes, those forty-five-degree cheekbones, that deep syrupy voice. 'I was within a few feet of her and it just blew me away. I took videos and photos and you can see my hands shaking,' Kai remembers. 'I mean, she just has a presence about her. I can't even explain it. I'm still speechless thinking about it.'

Kai met their girlfriend Shallie through a Cate Blanchett group chat. Cate fans might periodically tweet 'Retweet to join a group chat', meaning that you end up in a WhatsApp or Twitter group with a bunch of fans from all over the world. They've now been dating for nearly two years. At the beginning of 2020, Kai travelled from LA to go and live with Shallie in North Florida for a while. It's weird when you think about it: how Cate Blanchett, an actress who lives thousands of miles away across an ocean, is responsible for two people she has never met getting together. But such is the nature of fandom – there might be a person or group at its core, but it quickly flowers into something far beyond the original object of fanaticism.

Shallie, twenty-four, sees the Cate fandom as the queer community she'd long been craving. 'I grew up in a really small town in the South and was always kind of an oddball because none of my other friends were super into Cate Blanchett, and I was the only gay girl in my friend group,' she explains in a slow Southern drawl. 'So I created this Twitter account to meet more people and to kind of speak into the void of my love for this person, this actress, who is incredible. I never anticipated anything to come out of it and now I'm here, a year and a half later with this person that I met through Twitter who I'm stupid in love with. It's crazy.'

Most in the Cate fandom don't care that she's straight – it's not relevant, in the same way it's not relevant when the famous frontmen of bands have a long-term wife and kids, or when gay men drool over Timothée Chalamet or Nick Jonas. Part of stanning a person nearly always involves a heavy suspension of disbelief. It's all about the imagination, the spaces in between. When writing fanfiction, for instance, Cate fans will often include her husband Andrew as a character on the sidelines. In some, Cate and Andrew are in an open relationship. In others, they're headed for divorce. But IRL, Cate fans aren't particularly bothered about her private life. 'We joke about how we wish she was a lesbian, but at the end of the day, we know she's happy with Andrew and her family,' says Ren. 'We are too.'

Still, most of the queer fans I speak to are adamant that more LGBTQ roles ought to be given to LGBTQ actors. In 2018, when Cate Blanchett said she would 'fight to the death' for straight characters to play gay roles, a lot of her queer fans understandably bristled. It's one thing for queer viewers to decide who can tell their stories, but it's another for a straight actor to make that call for themselves. Especially when we consider that queer women winning prestigious awards is still extremely rare. The last queer woman to actually win an Oscar for a leading role was Jodie Foster in 1991 for *The Silence Of the Lambs* (although she wasn't out at the time). Any queer woman to be nominated for an Oscar since – Lady Gaga in 2018 for *A Star is Born* for instance – has done so off the back of an ultra hetero-leaning narrative. But queer women winning awards for queer roles? That's practically unheard of. And that's without even going into authentic trans representations of lesbianism or bisexuality, which are pretty much non-existent.

None of this seems to have dampened Cate's appeal among queer fans in the long run. I can understand the mixed feelings: you might stand by something on an intellectual and moral level, but your body is a ball of contradictions. Yeah, maybe the *Carol* leads should have gone to two lesbians. But also, let me perve over Blanchett's divine eyebrows and peachy hair and sculptural lips for a mo. It's also important to note here that perhaps we'd be having a different conversation if Cate's queer roles weren't executed with a certain amount of realism and attention to detail. When we're used to seeing straight women awkwardly pretend to finger each other on screen to appease the male gaze (see: *Chloe*, *Kissing Jessica Stein*, basically 85 per cent of 'lesbians' or 'bi women' having sex on screen), a realistic love scene still feels like a blessing. Kai agrees: 'I'm very much a proponent of LGBT people playing these roles, but at the same time she's a fabulous actress so why wouldn't you have her playing a queer role? If you're a stan, I guess you can look past that if you have an issue.'

Grace Perry, an American journalist, thinks our queer thirst for Cate Blanchett follows a tried and tested formula when it comes to straight women becoming lesbian or bi icons. In a 2019 article for *Buzzfeed*, she compares the Cate Blanchett hype to that of Rachel Weisz, who, following her queer roles in *Disobedience* and *The Favourite*, inspired a flurry of girls online demanding to be railed by this fifty-year-old straight woman. 'By the time Weisz had her big year in 2018, she fit neatly into an already well-established pattern: one, seemingly straight actor plays queer character, two, queer community thirsts over that queer character, three, queer community transitions thirst for queer character to thirst for straight actor, four, straight actor is deemed queer icon. Sometimes there's a three (b) phase, where a woman actor wears a suit on a red carpet.' The fantasy surrounding our lesbian or bi icons, then, becomes a little blurred. 'Do we worship Carol Aird, or do we worship Blanchett, or do we worship the internet version of Blanchett as documented in horny gay memes?' asks Perry. 'I don't even know anymore.'

I personally think our collective queer thirsting over Cate Blanchett extends far beyond Blanchett herself. Sure, she has the sort of eternal blue gaze that could freeze a human being and I'm pretty sure she came out of the womb wearing a fitted suit, but when we talk about the Blanchett fandom we're talking about much more than this one person who we don't even know. We're talking about a figure who exists at a far enough distance (straight, married, celebrity, A-lister) that we can safely project our feelings onto them without suffering the consequences. We're talking about a sounding board, a public space in which queer desire can be expressed loudly without shame. We're talking about how queer communities are formed, how they might be based around something arbitrary – an actor perhaps, or the love of a film, a band – but how their actual purpose is to bind people together via a sense of mutual understanding. We're talking about queer fantasy, queer yearning, the queer language of longing. The Cate fandom stands for all of these things. So does the film Carol. So do the many queer memes that cascade across our timelines on a regular basis. Like Perry said, it's difficult to know where one thing ends and another begins. In stanning Cate, then, we're mainly just celebrating queerness.

In May 2020, Cate Blanchett filmed an Instagram live with her best mate and frequent co-star Sarah Paulson for W magazine. The chat lasted around forty minutes, and was supposed to promote Mrs America, a drama miniseries in which they both appear. If you heard about this chat, though, you likely will have only heard about two seconds of it. The two seconds in which every single queer's heart stopped beating. The two seconds in which Cate Blanchett opened her mouth, stared into the iPhone camera lens and uttered the words, 'I'm a lesbian'. 'You're a lesbian?' replied Sarah Paulson, her face a mixture of shock and hope and delight. We were all Sarah Paulson in that moment. 'Apparently,' Cate Blanchett drawled back, blinking slowly.

Cate was just reading one of the on-screen Instagram comments aloud. She wasn't coming out to anybody. But the clip quickly did the rounds on Twitter and snowballed from there. One video was just Cate saying 'I'm a lesbian' on constant loop: 'I'm a lesbian, I'm a lesbian, I'm a lesbian.' The hysteria and joy surrounding Cate Blanchett saying those three magic words perhaps sums up the mechanics surrounding Cate Blanchett and queer fandom in general. Honestly no one cares if she's a lesbian. We know she's probably not. But there's a queer playfulness in us all joining together, just wanting and wishing and waiting to hear her say it.

CHAPTER SIX

Style

A s a small child, I only wanted to wear fairy dresses. Pink ones. White ones. Alien green. Wings attached to my back with an elastic band. Wands made out of plastic, wands with batteries in them that went *brrrriiiiinggg* when you swished them, wands with glittery stars tacked to the end with cheap glue. Before we left the house, Mum would present me with a variety of coloured jeans that she had bought from a charity shop. 'Yuck,' I would say, eyeballing these stiff, boyish items. 'Do you want to just wear your fairy dress then?' she would laugh. And out the door we would go – me in pink, white or green – the adjacent fairy accessories shoved chaotically into her handbag.

But as I grew up, something changed, something that I barely noticed at the time. The tiny bows on my vests started to feel stuffy ('Aaaaaawww,' said one teaching assistant when she noticed a pink bow poking out of my T-shirt. Aged nine, I glowered, wanting to punch her). The skirts I was dressed in began to feel like weird bandages wrapped around boyish legs. And I noticed myself eyeing up boys' clothes with something akin to jealousy, or want: The jeans, they sat so nicely on the hips, and the cuffs of those jeans, they rested so casually on the trainers. The T-shirts – plain and loose-hanging and muted – looked right. Being pulled around the girls' section of H&M by the hand – among Groovy Chick crop tops, sequin-studded jeans – I felt I was in the wrong clothes. They were in my clothes. The unfairness of it sat stiffly in my gut.

By the time I was twelve, I had rejected girls' clothes entirely and wore my hair chin-length and bedraggled, like the boys at school. Passers-by would question my gender. 'Are you a boy or a girl?' kids would ask straightforwardly, mouth agape. Others would whisper, pointing to the small mounds under my T-shirt: 'She's a girl, look, she has boobs.' I felt both irritated and pleased by the ambiguity of my appearance. I knew I was a girl because I felt like a girl, mostly, whatever that meant – this wasn't full on gender dysphoria – but my gender also felt complicated, anomalous, swaying in the wind. 'Girl,' I would whisper back, or, sometimes, 'Boy.' Whichever child had asked would nod back, solemnly.

I didn't walk or talk 'like a girl' either. My grandma thought it was because I'd been hanging around skate parks. 'You've picked up that swagger,' she would say in the car ride home, skateboard rattling in the car boot. 'You walk like you have something stuck between your legs.' What I couldn't explain to her was that this was just how my body moved; of its own accord.

Even as I entered early teenagerhood, the way I held myself didn't budge. I wore low-hanging jeans and scuffed skate train-ers, oversized T-shirts that sagged around my body like a flag. Those my age didn't care or comment. Boys who shared my interests (skateboarding, music) asked me out via handwritten notes passed across school desks. And then we would walk around, holding hands, looking like two boys from behind. 'Sometimes I think I fancy you,' a straight best friend confessed to me once, her lip-glossed mouth opening in self-surprise. I thought I knew what she meant. She didn't fancy me, she fancied the boyness of me, the way I dressed like her boyfriends. It was confusing for me too.

But later, when we became more conscious of our bodies, when we began using them, my appearance didn't seem to fly under the radar in quite the same way. The vibe was clear: Why didn't I accentuate my new curves? Why wasn't I prettier, more made up? Why didn't I wear tight denim skirts at house parties and grind by the speakers to Flo Rida singing about 'Apple Bottom jeans' like a normal teenage girl instead of scabbing my knees up on the concrete outside? At this point I didn't consider myself queer, but I was slowly becoming a repellent to teenage boys anyway. Something about me wasn't quite right. Many years later, upon reading *Female Masculinity*, I learned that this change in tide during adolescence is a pattern that repeats itself. 'Teenage tomboyism presents a problem and tends to be subject to the most severe efforts to reorientate,' Jack Halberstam writes. 'We could say that tomboyism is tolerated as long as the child remains prepubescent; as soon as puberty begins, however, the full force of gender conformity descends on the girl.'

Any 'boyishness' was rattled out of me then, pushed into the ether as I crammed myself into Primark push-up bras and bright bodycon skirts. This is something that happens to everyone, obviously, not just queer women. Gender conformity comes for us all, regardless of gender or orientation. And for trans people, especially, this experience can be deeply destabilising, oppressive in ways that only trans people have a right to describe. Within the trans community, non-binary people face their own unique struggles when it comes to being shoved into one gender box or the other, presentation-wise. Either way, if you're not heterosexual, the bind of gender norms can feel extra tight because it's so intertwined with how desirable you are to the opposite sex. For anyone who's not a cis man, the male gaze is draped around you like an invisible curtain as soon as you're read as 'woman': dress yourself a certain way or else no man will ever love you, and what would be the point of you then?

Looking at photos from around this time feels almost dysphoric. Foundation and long, straightened hair. Heels and opaque, clinging tights. During one memorable boat trip – for our school's year-end prom, charging up the River Thames – I arrived wearing Vivienne Westwood heels I had saved up for, paired with a dress resembling a bulbous, holographic lampshade. By the end of the trip I had pulled the dress down, replaced it with a Melvins T-shirt, removed my heels so that I was barefoot. My discomfort was palpable, volumised in the sticky heat of the boat. 'You look very . . . Camden Market?' joked one French teacher, winking at me. I ignored him, disappearing to drink warm Red Stripe alone in the swaying boat toilets. *What a pile of shit*, I thought, looking down at my ripped lampshade dress and wondering if life would feel like this forever. Afterwards I flung the heels into the water. They suddenly looked to me like stupid hooves.

I'm not the only queer woman to share this experience of feeling somehow pressured into dressing 'like a straight girl' in the years before coming out. Others I speak to relay similar memories. My friend Shauna likes to send me photos of her at school or uni, looking unrecognisable with long hair and lipstick and miniskirts, so that we can marvel at our queer glow-ups together (sometimes she still wears lipstick and miniskirts, but on her own terms, rather than as a method of 'disguise'). Another friend of mine, a self-described butch woman, spent her school years dressed almost exactly like Diana Vickers from series five of *The X Factor* (backcombed hair, matte mousse lips). These days, you'd be hard-pressed to find her in anything other than jeans,

T-shirts and work boots. 'I wish I'd embraced my butchness sooner,' she told me once, shrugging. 'It would have saved me a lot of discomfort.'

Years after school, once I'd stepped into my queerness, it wasn't just a relief in a romantic or sexual sense – it was a relief in an aesthetic sense too. I no longer cared about being coded as queer, because I am queer – and queer aesthetics have no problem operating outside of gender norms. I no longer cared about attracting men because it was irrelevant. Suddenly, my hair could be any style. My clothes functional, comfortable. Or else my style could be femme, lipsticked, soft-edged. Either way was fine, role switching could be fun. Style tastes differently once heterosexual male desire is taken out of the equation. I would imagine the same might apply to straight people; I would imagine it applies to everyone. But within queerness I found the freedom to ditch long-standing gendered modes of expression. I embraced queer ones instead: autonomy, playfulness, the deep rich warmth of freedom.

When I have conversations with other queer women, they recall similar revelations. Experiences in which them coming out (to themselves or others) resulted in an external shift, a 'freeing up' in terms of gender expression and expectation. Some started wearing more masculine clothes because they didn't feel the need to be 'straight-passing' anymore. 'I used to be so self-conscious of looking "stereotypically gay" that I went the opposite, being super typically femme and "straight-looking" . . . Now I have no problem with it because I am gay and I want people to know about it,' says twenty-four-year-old Sally. Caitlin, twenty, says a similar thing. 'I've learned that "looking gay" isn't a bad thing . . . Like, so what if men don't like that I don't shave and I wear earrings with tiny vibrators on them? They're not the target audience."

Others told me the opposite. They used to feel uncomfortable wearing feminine clothes in case they were coded as straight. But once they came out, those codes didn't feel so stifling. Femininity was to be explored, embraced. 'Once I came to terms with my own sexuality, I actually started wearing more feminine clothes,' explains twenty-two-year-old Laura. 'Now I know that I'm not dressing up to please men, I wear make-up or dresses and feel comfortable with it. The downside is that girls always think I'm straight, which is a pain in the ass.' Shona, twenty-two, tells me that coming out as bisexual freed up her style because she felt like she could never win anyway – people would assume she was either gay or straight regardless. So she took things into her own hands. 'I felt more comfortable picking clothes that I actually liked rather than what people thought I should wear.'

Of course, the fashion choices of queer women have never just been about shaking off the male gaze, where relevant. They're also about embracing and inviting the female gaze, or else simply dressing for yourself, on your own terms. But how does that manifest? What does that look like? Most queer women will tell you that they can recognise another queer woman on the street when they see one (or like to think so) but find it harder to outline exactly why and what it is they're looking for. The lesbian/bi aesthetic exists – energetically, unquestionably, a force of its own – but how might we recognise it and how exactly have queer women established such a specific yet ephemeral mode of style over years, decades and even centuries?

§

For a long time, the idea of a lesbian or bi aesthetic was known and loved among queer women and misunderstood or joked about everywhere else. In mainstream pop culture – up until the

2010s at least – we were regularly portrayed as dowdy and boring, unglamorous and masculine, traipsing around in flannel shirts and Birkenstocks and shapeless clothing items made out of recyclable materials (think Carol and Susan's drab wedding guests in *Friends*, hairy-legged Patty coming out as gay in *The Simpsons*, the lesbian undertones of monobrowed Miss Trunchbull in *Matilda* with her weird sweatshirts and belts). As Inge Blackman and Kathryn Perry wrote in their essay 'Skirting the Issue: Lesbian Fashion for the 1990s' in the spring 1990 issue of *Feminist Review*: 'The contemporary lesbian is considered to be "congenitally" unfashionable; too busy propping up Havelock Ellis's eternal mantlepiece, pipe in hand, gently flicking ash off her tweeds, to spare a thought for trend.' Queer historian Karen Tongson went as far as to joke that most people viewed the term 'lesbian aesthetics' as words that cancel each other out: 'a conceptual incompatibility at best, a humorous oxymoron at worst.'

But queer women have always had style. In fact, our cultural history is so intertwined with aesthetics that the many ways in which we present and hold ourselves have been recognised as a complex organising system – and a mode of dissent – with longstanding categories and specifications.

The terms 'butch' and 'femme' are the most well-known and thrown around of these aesthetic markers. Some claim that these identities were historically a way of organising same-sex relationships in a way that mirrored traditional heterosexual power dynamics (with the butch taking on the active, dominant role of the man and the femme taking on the passive, submissive role of the woman), while others have argued that they should be recognised as something entirely independent, as identities distinct to queer culture, maybe even in direct opposition to heteronormativity. Either way, I think theorist Gayle Rubin defines it most succinctly: 'Butch is the lesbian vernacular term for women who are more comfortable with masculine gender codes, styles or identities than with feminine ones.' And as Jack Halberstam points out in *Female Masculinity*, 'masculinity' needn't be conflated with the 'male' body. They are two separate things. Culturally associated, sure, but separate.

'Butch–femme' identities have a rich and complicated back-story in the West. Queer historians argue about the whats, whens and whys, but everyone agrees that there are clear examples of butches and femmes dating back to the 1920s and 1930s at least, with origins in working-class lesbian bars and house parties – often a mix of both Black and white people. Photos from around this time are gorgeous and astonishing – women with slicked-back hair, wide-legged trousers and belts, arms slung around soft-faced girls in floor-length dresses and pearls. Out of context, these butch queers could have been from any place, any era: a club night in New York or Berlin somewhere, cropped hair and androgynous clothes, one eyebrow cocked, a time-defying swagger.

By the 1950s and 1960s, the butch–femme style system was in full swing, although those who adhered remained outsiders among straight society. Notoriously in the United States, up until the 1980s at least, women were required by law to wear at least three items of clothing conventionally associated with the gender they were assigned with at birth. This meant that – while cis, femme lesbians might pass as straight – the butch identity consistently held anti-establishment power, a danger that persisted by virtue of being visible, especially if you were also a person of colour and/or working class. Law enforcement would use such regulations as an excuse to raid LGBTQ bars constantly (a fact which, aside from the persecution of queer women, also majorly tyrannized trans communities specifically. In essence, these laws were designed to clamp down and oppress any inkling of gender freedom among anyone who wasn't cis or straight).

In her 1982 autobiography *Zami: A New Spelling Of My Name*, poet and activist Audre Lorde remembers her own experiences of that era: 'There were always rumours of plain-clothes women circulating among us, looking for gay girls with fewer than three pieces of female attire. This was enough to get you arrested for transvestism, which was illegal. Or so the rumours went. Most of the women we knew were always careful to put on a bra, underpants and some other feminine article. No sense playing with fire.'

Once the 1970s landed, middle class (mainly white) lesbian feminists also took aim at the butch–femme binary. They viewed it as an artificial impersonation of heterosexist ideals, as a habit perpetuated by rough-edged uneducated working-class lesbians who hung around in bars giving other queer women a bad rep. 'Feminists' of this ilk believed that by casting off butch–femme stereotypes, lesbian and bi women would be free from patriarchal constraints. However, as Jack Halberstam points out, the suppression of these identities 'further erased an elaborate and carefully scripted language of desire that butch and femme dykes had produced in response to dominant culture's attempts to wipe them out'. In essence, the butch aesthetic was being attacked from all angles: too assimilative for the gays and too deviant for the straights.

What some middle-class lesbian feminists seemed to get wrong were the complexities and subtleties that exist within the butch–femme spectrum. It isn't a limited binary – cheap copies of 'man' and 'woman' – but instead the opposite, everything in between. Soft butches and hard femmes. Stone butches and pillow princesses. Diesel dykes and bois. Bull daggers and bull dykes and studs (the latter terms being born from Black and Latinx lesbian communities in Harlem). Each term expressing a variant on style, how a queer person holds themselves, dresses or even – in some cases – has sex. Trans-masculine people, too, have often identified within these terms (although it's worth pointing out here that some trans men also reject the term 'butch' due to its historical associations with lesbianism). The dismissal of this language by feminists was, then, an erasure of working-class and racial cultural history, an erasure of how minority groups injected nuance into the diversities that exist within gender and queer desire. In rejecting the butch–femme spectrum because they believed it fed into heterosexual structures, they failed to recognise that they were viewing queer language through a rigidly heteronormative lens.

Despite such attacks, queers have consistently returned to the butch–femme aesthetic – though the codes have shifted and evolved over the years. The late 1980s and 1990s saw butchness and femmeness return with added aplomb. This was the era of Judith Butler's *Gender Trouble*. Of Leslie Feinberg's *Stone Butch Blues*. Of Ellen DeGeneres coming out on primetime TV in a tailored suit and short hair. Of Cindy Crawford draped around k.d. lang on the cover of *Vanity Fair*. Of Missy Elliott donning vests, chains, suits and work boots. Butchness in particular, as a word encompassing style and sexuality and gender expression, came to be viewed as a little less static throughout these later eras too. 'Not every butch has short hair, can change a tire, desires a femme. Some butches are bottoms,' wrote Kerry Manders in the *New York Times*. 'Some butches are bi. Some butches are boys.'

Eventually even the straight world began to embrace a certain dykey look and swagger. Sporty Spice with her tribal armband tatts, trainers and vests. TLC with Tommy Hilfiger boxers poking out of loose Champion trackies. Winona Ryder in baggy suit-jackets and bandanas. Supermodel Erin O'Connor posing for Moschino in a full drag king get-up, ruffled shirt with the collar popped up. By the time the twentieth century came to a close, what had once been so derided in relation to lesbian and bi communities was drip, drip, dripping into mainstream culture so subtly that it barely even registered as an association at all. For a group of people who have, for so long, been stereotyped as purposefully and painfully 'unfashionable', our influence on mainstream fashion as a whole can look fundamentally undeniable.

§

Today, queer women's style is a little harder to define than the butch–femme systems of the last century – although it is by no means divorced. When I do a quick shout-out on Instagram asking what queer codes exist among women today, I get a variety of responses. Short fringes and thumb rings. Blazers and wide-legged trousers. Vests and DIY mullets and snakeskin Birkenstocks. Ugly shoes and socks and slicked-back hair. Button-up shirts and long, heavy-duty trench coats. Grey denim. Silver chains. Carabiner keyrings and Dickies. Undercuts. Fleeces and cord trousers and weird hats. Bold make-up, mismatched colours. One responder points out how any article along the lines of 'Men Hate It When Girls Wear This!' is usually an indicator of brilliant queer style choices. In a piece published for the *Telegraph* in 2017, for instance, the writer cites clogs and leather trousers and oversized jumpers as being total man repellents. Maybe it's a coincidence that those are all items I have searched for on Depop over the past two years.

Written down, the aforementioned queer style codes look almost random (what has a trench coat got to do with carabiner keyrings? What has a thumb ring got to do with socks?). But there's a clear thread that travels between them. Queer style is not necessarily interested in the male gaze. Queer style is not necessarily interested in gendered norms. Queer style is not necessarily interested in what is conventionally deemed 'ugly', because 'ugliness' itself is based on heteronormative, Western standards of beauty (a fleece might be considered 'ugly', for example, because women are traditionally encouraged to show off particular sections of their body and look sexy or submissive, which the fleece doesn't scream). When we bear all of that in mind, the aforementioned clothing items actually start to make a lot more sense together. We'll wear a fleece because we like the look of it. And if it's a really ugly fleece? Even better. Because ugliness means we're pushing up against what that even means.

We can see this idea play out with the mullet, a hairstyle that is particularly popular among dykes and bi girls across London, Bushwick, Melbourne and literally any area containing more than one art gallery and coffee shop. I think the mullet is gorgeous – weird, bold, like two haircuts cut 'n' pasted into one – but over the decades it also became symbolic of everything ridiculous and oddball. The reasons for this are easy to trace: the hairstyle was popular among glam rock punks in the 1970s as a way of blending masculine and feminine gender codes and was therefore subversive. It was then popular among tacky pop stars in the 1980s, whereby it was considered cheesy and gauche. And it's always been associated with cowboys, country music fans, redneck dudes in dive bars in outback towns across Australia and the US, giving it classist connotations. In the other words, the mullet stood for bad taste in the mainstream. It wasn't how a 'pretty girl' would style her hair. So from the very beginning, the mullet has also been adopted by hordes and hordes of queer girls as a way of saying 'fuck you' and 'look at me'. 'I absolutely think it's a lesbian haircut because it's always my hair that gives me away,' says one woman in the 2001 documentary *American Mullet*. 'It's the dyke cut, the lesbian cut, it's butch.'

Jemima Bradley, a twenty-one-year-old hairdresser responsible for pretty much every mullet you see on queer kids and art weirdos around London today, tells me that she's always viewed the haircut as an expression of queer identity: 'In the 1970s, lesbians were one of the first to take on the style to show their dykeness.' Today, queer women wear mullets for the same reasons: 'More recently, it became a way of identifying with who's queer, it became a community statement. It's about androgyny, not conforming to a certain gender, not conforming to society.' Essentially, queer women's styles become so because they push back against ideas of how women should dress, how we should behave. And then as a result they become a way of signalling queerness.

One of my favourite theories about queer women's style is that it's not just preoccupied with the body, but with what the body can do. This is where the female gaze comes into play, and where more 'practical' or 'functional' clothing items can be seen as being intimately bound up with queer desire. Take the plain white vest, for example, which, throughout pop culture, has long been considered the perennial lesbian and bi fashion item (see: the film poster for *Bound* (1996), model Jenny Shimizu throughout the entirety of the nineties, the many subjects of photographer Catherine Opie; literally any lesbian or bi girl with no bra and a silver chain on Instagram).

The vest has historically been associated with working-class men, with movement, with doing. You can do anything in a vest – fix a car, change a tyre, go for a run – while also hinting at the skin underneath. Depending on the shape of the vest and the vibe of its wearer, the vest can say anything from 'I'm really good with a hammer and some flatpack IKEA furniture' to 'I'm really good with my hands, and by extension fingering'. In other words, the right vest worn in the right way says, 'I know exactly how to want and touch another woman.' Vests can give off horny energy, or they can give off practical energy, but fundamentally, they can give off both – which is what makes them especially dykey. It's what makes keys dykey. It's what makes jeans dykey too.

The idea that something can look 'dykey' is important when it comes to signalling. When we still often assume people's straightness until they tell us otherwise, queer codes invite us to read between the lines, especially when we're not in overtly queer spaces. Obviously this is not a fail-safe system – just because that woman in the nut milk section of the off-licence has a Patti Smith mullet and really ugly cords does not automatically mean she likes going down on other women – but there's something to be said about the subtle and complex ways in which women signal their queerness to one another. I own about twenty different white vests because they're comfortable, yes, but also maybe subconsciously because they read as queer. 'It's not only a uniform, but a Freemason's handshake,' wrote lesbian journalist Sophie Wilkinson in the *Guardian* in 2015. 'It's how we could tell the queer from the straight.'

Sometimes queer signifiers can be dangerous. I've lost count of the number of times I've been told I 'look like a lesbian' as if that's a bad thing, and you'd be hard-pressed to find a queer person who dresses visibly queer and hasn't been heckled on the street. In the West we might be past the point at which women are being arrested for failing to wear three items of 'women's' clothing, but homo-phobic attacks based on appearance are still a regular occurrence: In January 2020, a twenty-year-old woman in Sunderland was pushed to the ground and punched in the head by two men for what she looked like. 'I do look like a boy and I do act like a boy and there is no femininity about me at all,' she said following the attack. Later, in August 2020, a forty-five-year-old woman was attacked in a park in Wales while walking her dog after two men took aim at her T-shirt and tattoos. Both women said that this was not the first time they had been assaulted for similar reasons.

It's also worth pointing out here that while the above examples are about two lesbians, any attack based on gender nonconformity is, at its root, a transphobic attack. These aren't attacks on 'style' so much as they're attacks on any visible divergence from cisnormative ideals. This violence also isn't rare and it isn't vague and it isn't a thing of the past – it is targeted and specific and happening currently. In 2020, for example, at least 350 trans people were murdered globally, with 38 per cent of those murders occurring in the streets. In the US alone, 79 per cent of the aforementioned murders were of trans people of colour. When looking at statistics like these, a grim picture emerges, one which is as clear as day: gender norms aren't just uncomfortable. They also actively promote violence and are consistently compounded by racism.

When it come to lesbian and bi style specifically, clothes can still indicate outsider and insider status. For me personally – a cis, white woman – it's not a conscious thing. I don't go around looking for girls with short fringes and septum rings and stick 'n' poke tattoos reading 'lezzie'. But if I find myself surrounded by those people, I'll generally feel more at ease than when I'm in an office setting, maybe, or in a pub full of straight guys. For people of colour, this feeling can obviously be even more pronounced. One queer Muslim woman from Pakistan tells me that she feels as though she's constantly holding her breath in most public spaces. It's only when she's in a space full of other queer Muslims that she breathes out, relaxes for a moment.

Queer women's style might be easy to recognise, but it's often been hard to put into words – especially considering it's as much to do with an item of clothing as it is with how it's worn. But in 2018, the writer Mikaella Clements attempted to give the aesthetic a name: 'dyke camp'. In a piece titled 'Notes On Dyke Camp' for the now defunct culture website *The Outline*, Clements sketches out a working theory: 'Dyke camp overlaps with camp in some areas, certainly. But in others it is completely different; it has its own electric vision. If camp is the love of the unnatural, dyke camp is the love of the ultra-natural, of nature built up and reclaimed, of clothes that could be extensions of the body, of desire made obsessive, of lesbian gestures or mannerisms maximized by a thousand.'

Clements tells me over the phone that she chose the term 'dyke camp' to explain a look that is so familiar to lesbian and bi women but isn't often expressed: 'Like a lot of lesbians, I point at things a lot and say "that's so dykey, that's really dykey" but it felt like that adjective wasn't enough to describe it anymore. It had to be a particular aesthetic, a particular take.' In the piece, she points to the queer female gaze as being integral to dyke camp: 'If straight women put on public displays of lesbianism for male attention, dyke camp takes private lesbian contact and makes it public – for other women,' she writes, adding that, 'dyke camp is less about having a hot body, and more about knowing how to use it. It's why dyke camp is so often rooted in swagger, in cockiness.'

Over the past few years, we've seen dyke camp – aka the queer female gaze – slowly trickling into mainstream pop culture with increasing regularity. Just take a look around and you'll notice it: Kate McKinnon in a popped collar, licking her gun before shooting it in *Ghostbusters*. Blake Lively in a fitted suit and tie, leaning across and kissing the startled face of Anna Kendrick in *A Simple Favour*. St. Vincent with greased-back hair, clutching her guitar like a lover. Kehlani with a cigarette resting between two tattooed fingers, blowing smoke into the sky. Spanish model Alba Galocha in loose-hanging jeans and a turtleneck, arms resting casually across a balcony. The difference between this and the optics of t.A.T.u for instance, or Madonna and Britney at the VMAs, is that their eroticism is not like the eroticism you might see in straight porn, where two female bodies are lesbian or bi simply because they're making out. Instead, it's an eroticism that says: I have a body and I know how to use it. The queer gaze is about power and desire and movement, rather than what anyone looks like through the eyes of straight men.

Just as the queer gaze has been trickling into the mainstream, so too have queer style codes – meaning they aren't necessarily always queer style codes anymore. Throughout the latter 2010s especially, gender-neutral fashion saw a massive uptick in ubiquity. Just take a look at the runways of Gucci and Marc Jacobs, of Saint Laurent and JW Anderson, of Louis Vuitton and Celine. Take a look at the surge in popularity of androgynous and gender-blurring labels like Ashley Williams and Public School and Charles Jeffrey's Loverboy. It's now much more 'normal' – whatever that means – to see male models draped in fierce dresses and billowing skirts and women striding in bold, tailored unisex suits. Not just on the runway, but also among the stars: Who would have thought, a decade ago, that we'd end up witnessing the likes of Young Thug, Jaden Smith and Harry Styles gracing magazine covers and red carpets in spectacular dresses, ruffles spilling dramatically around their bodies like cream on a cake?

This isn't just a high-fashion thing either – we've seen a recent shift on the high street too. Selfridges, H&M, Zara: these are all mainstream retailers that have launched gender-neutral collections in the latter 2010s. These are shops that your hetero aunt and uncle might pop into to get Christmas presents for the family, where your nan might find a nice new cardigan. Their move towards unisex clothing, then, signals a wider shift in relation to gender presentation. Obviously gender-neutral fashion is not a new thing, and it's not always been a queer thing either: straight, cis people have experimented with womenswear and menswear throughout history too (Prince, David Bowie, Patti Smith, I could go on). But definitions of femininity and masculinity are clearly becoming less divorced from gender for everyone – not just for queer folk.

Elsewhere, even straight A-listers are starting to look a bit dykey. Take the mullet, for example, which has quickly spread from the queer and punk underground to the red carpet. We've got Rihanna, and Maisie Williams, and Leigh-Anne Pinnock of Little Mix rocking mullets these days. We've got Gigi Hadid sporting one on the cover of *Vogue Mexico*. We've got Miley Cyrus – who is pansexual, yes, but who is also a good indicator of the American mainstream – in a shaggy Bushwick mullet, vest and Levi jeans, looking like every single girl off Tinder who's ever broken my heart. Stepping outside of sexuality for a moment, this is an interesting shift for fashion. Maybe people of all genders and sexualities are becoming less afraid to take risks, maybe the male gaze is starting to lose its potency for everyone.

Valerie Steele, a renowned American fashion historian and curator, also thinks that clothes might look a bit 'dykier' these days because fashion in general has got more casual, less flamboyant. 'I think there was a casualisation across fashion for everybody, and that's brought back a sense that a lot of utilitarian clothes are more authentic than fashion-y clothes,' she explains over the phone from New York. 'People are more willing or indeed happy to be associated with wearing things like jumpsuits, Birkenstocks, Doc Martens. These somehow seem more authentic than a high-fashion shoe or something.'

All of the above has had a knock-on effect when it comes to queer signalling. Where you once might have assumed that the girl behind the supermarket checkout with the razor-cut fringe and customised men's jeans was a fellow lez, she's now just as likely to be another young alt with a Depop account. While some of this can be attributed to current fashion trends, it also points to the fact that young people in particular aren't so bothered about gendered norms, nor rigid ideas about sexuality. With 60 per cent of Generation Z shopping across gendered sections, the idea that a butch-looking woman is likely to be gay or bi is starting to feel almost old-fashioned. As gender and sexual binaries become blurred, so too do the fashion choices that used to represent them.

For lesbian and bi women, this evolution might feel faintly threatening. How is anyone supposed to express their queerness if everyone is starting to look a bit queer? 'What was once a queer-owned style has shifted to the mainstream, being appropriated by straight women to the point that it's now impossible to infer a sexual orientation from the way a woman dresses,' wrote Sophie Wilkinson in the aforementioned *Guardian* piece. Dressing 'like a lesbian' might have been thrown around as an insult, but it was also a point of pride, a way of sticking your finger up to a world that consistently tried to erase you. If everyone and their sister are starting to wear big baggy tees and ugly Crocs and tailored suit trousers, how are we supposed to sign-post our difference, our pride?

It can also feel jarring to see straight A-listers celebrated for trends that originated in queer communities: queer and trans people are still experiencing violence based on their appearance, yet Harry Styles gets praise for wearing a designer dress once? But the freeing up of gendered norms can also be viewed as a positive step forward for everyone – these two opinions can exist in tandem. We can feel protective of lesbian and bi fashion histories – of the many radical ways in which we naturally expressed ourselves and still do – while also feeling excited for a future in which young people no longer feel confined to the style prisons of the past. If I ever have kids I hope they grow up wearing whatever they feel like, regardless of their gender identity or who they fall in love with.

I often wonder what my teenage years would have felt like had I been born even just ten years later. I spent a long time feeling uncomfortable in my own skin – like an alien to my gender – confused as to why certain clothes simply didn't sit right on my body. It took me years to finally feel at ease with the way I presented, and while some of that was down to growing into adulthood, as we all do eventually, a lot of it was down to stepping into my queerness and shaking off a whole load of internalised heteronormativity. Had I known earlier that gender norms are a construct, that there's no right or wrong way to present, maybe I'd have moved throughout the world a little lighter back then. Maybe I'd have saved the eighty pounds I spent on those Vivienne Westwood heels too. Or maybe I'd have actually enjoyed wearing them.

This is an era in which gender binaries are becoming blurred, in which style is becoming more playful, in which people's clothes don't necessarily say anything about their sexual preference or gender. It's hard to say what the queer codes of tomorrow will look like, whether they will even exist, or whether they will even need to. This is the age of being constantly online, after all, in which a gazillion different versions of identity and style and aesthetics exist simultaneously on our grids and timelines and reels. This is a time in which we have never been more divorced from our bodies, our clothes, the physical manifestation of our identities.

Indeed, we can't ever properly predict the future. But if there's one place that might give us a clue, that might tell us where queer codes and queer culture in general might be headed, it is surely the great mass sitting right in front of us: the internet.

CHAPTER SEVEN

The Internet

Cole resembles a teenage Justin Bieber. Her floppy hair is usually divided into two colours – black and pink, black and blue, black and bleached – and in her videos she wears zipped hoodies and vests, chains and long sleeves with neon prints. She has the kind of youthful cheek-boned androgyny that makes modelling agencies trip over each other, and the kind of bored, sullen eyes that make other teenagers do the same. Cole is seventeen years old and has over 230,000 followers on TikTok and counting. '17! Lesbian!' reads her bio. 'I do it for the girls 'n' the gays, that's it.'

Like most clips on the video-sharing app, Cole's are hard to explain to those who aren't already well versed in the internet miasma. They sit somewhere between selfies, comedy sketches, music videos and memes, with their own surreal, in-joke humour and blink-or-you'll-miss-it rhythm distinct to TikTok. But mainly people come for the gay content and, I'd imagine, because she looks like a gothy poster boy. 'Lesbians getting shown their friend's boyfriends' reads one text overlay, while she play-acts pretending to be interested. 'Me panicking because it's February 13th and I haven't got my girlfriend anything for Valentine's Day' reads another, her head resting on a pillow, bathed in pink light. Then the colours change. 'Oh wait, I don't have a gf. K I sneep.' The comments are all variations of the same thing: *Hi I'm ur new gf. I'll be ya gf. What about me? Be mine?*

Cole isn't the only prolific lesbian/gay/bi teen on TikTok. Nor is she a rarity. If you spend even a couple of hours scrolling through one specific corner of TikTok, the algorithm starts feeding you queer content, like a chef fixing up your favourite meal based on you once mentioning a few ingredients.

Through Cole I find other TikTok users like Hope, a nineteen-year-old with 400,000 followers. Their short shaggy hair is also divided into two colours – black and blond – paired with boyish clothes that wouldn't look amiss in a nineties Larry Clark movie. Nine times out of ten, their videos have a queer theme. 'Me @ any girl I catch feelings for' reads a caption, with Hope passionately lip-synching the words to Fitz and The Tantrums' indie pop song 'Out Of My League' while in their car. In another they're staring at you down the camera lens, singing a slowed down version of Katy Perry's 'I Kissed A Girl'. The comments from other teens are littered with other teens guessing whether they're a 'top' or a 'bottom' (gay terms used to describe who the 'givers' and 'receivers' are in sex) based on their movements alone – a theme I quickly learn is common among queer TikTok: *Only time I've ever seen top energy* (685 likes), *Bottom* (1,221 likes), *AHAHA bottom* (402 likes).

Lesbian couples are especially popular on TikTok. Karin and Skyler have close to a million followers, a number matched only by their one million YouTube subscribers. Like a lot of TikTok's bigger names, they're so conventionally good looking it's almost painful: straight white teeth, glowing skin, gym-taut stomachs, a sober fresh American energy. Karin dresses in more masc clothes, with a bandana or backwards cap, hair tied up to reveal an undercut, while Skyler looks like a Disney princess in baggy sweats and crop tops. Together they do casual dance routines in front of the camera, take part in TikTok challenges, or else just kiss, looking into each other's eyes, the ever-invisible iPhone propped out-of-view in someone's hand. Most videos have some variation of the hashtag #couplegoals in the caption and the comments, from young queers mainly, seem to agree: *Ugh you guys are too cute*, one gushes. *You guys will forever be my favourite couple*, writes another. *You inspired me so much to come out! Thank you for everything.* Heart-eye emojis scatter the screen.

Once you start scrolling, it's hard to stop. I had initially set up a TikTok account for research, to see how queer online spaces had changed since I was a teenager. But before long I was checking it purely for entertainment, distraction, procrastination. I'd lie there with my eyes fixed on the tiny luminous rectangle until one, two in the morning, swiping gormlessly through random people's bedrooms, hastily turning down the volume whenever some kind of trap Spongebob hybrid mix blurted out of the tinny speakers while my girlfriend snored quietly beside me. In my late twenties, I feel a little too old for TikTok – roughly 41 per cent of TikTok users are aged between sixteen and twenty-four, and the mood definitely leans towards 'teen', although that has recently been changing. But there's no denying that the platform is addictive, moreish from a distance. Even its name – TikTok – brings to mind Disney's *Peter Pan* character Tick-Tock the crocodile, whose incessant ticking and tocking haunts Captain Hook to near madness, so unable is he to shake the sound from his head.

For all their sexual innuendo and talk of tops and bottoms, the vibe among queer teens on TikTok is distinctly wholesome. When I close my eyes and think back to being sixteen, I picture (and cringe at) all the Facebook albums of me and my friends falling over each other, joints sticking out of spotty faces, digital camera snaps of someone in a denim skirt and UGG boots being sick in a parent's flower pot after bombing mephedrone, never thinking for a moment that any of these photos might live on. But the teens on TikTok seem publicly healthier somehow, more straight-edged, well put together. They also seem culturally clued-up in ways we weren't – at least among certain corners (as with any online platform, there are darker sides to TikTok too). They educate each other on pronouns, profess they'll block anyone who uses homophobic, transphobic or racist language and make videos acknowledging the reality of bi erasure. Queerness on TikTok is an ongoing conversation, not just an orientation. Obviously, I don't know what teenagers get up to beyond what I see on the screen – and if I remember being under twenty-one correctly, adults rarely knew the half of it. But the onus among a lot of teens on TikTok appears, to me at least, less about being a fuck-up and more about having a moral compass (and if you're the former, at least having the language to talk about it).

When TikTok first launched in 2017 in China – then in 2018 throughout the rest of the world – it very swiftly became a lot of young adults' preferred choice of social media. Facebook had long been for boomers posting pics of their nieces and nephews alongside rabid fake news about Brexit and 5G conspiracy theories. Twitter was for twitchy media millennials and angry-reply guys, more interested in snarling 'hot takes' than fun challenges where you could also flaunt your looks. Instagram, while still prolific and aesthetic-based, was becoming less private, with older generations making their own accounts and following family members. I can imagine it being difficult for a young person to build an online identity – or try new ones out for size – when they've got their Auntie Lisa posting beneath their thirst traps: 'Nice top sweetie! Is it new? Lisa x'. And so, with the similarly youth-led Snapchat biting at its heels, TikTok gained a reputation for being the app that hordes of young people were obsessed with, but that others didn't quite understand. By 2020, in figures that most start-ups can only dream of, TikTok had around 800 million monthly active users – more than double that of both Snapchat and Twitter and nearly as much as Instagram.

As with any online space that still retains a certain degree of privacy from the prying eyes of adults and outsiders, TikTok users have cultivated their own thriving queer community. A large subsection of them are young queer women, a phenomenon that has given rise to the oft-used term 'TikTok lesbian', which is to say, any lesbian on TikTok. The algorithm-led format means that queer kids can find each other without having to do much active looking. A few rainbow flags and #lesbian or #bi searches will lead you to more of the same. And the way it functions, scrolling up to the next clip as soon as one seconds-long clip ends, means that you become engulfed in endless content very quickly. The result is less an organically cultivated queer scene in the way of, say, IRL gay clubs (which many young people might not enjoy or have access to) or certain niche online forums, and more a case of, if you want to find other LGBTQ kids, here they all are. Join us.

Cole is based in Toronto, Canada. She tells me that at first she thought TikTok was 'kind of cringy'; she only joined as a joke. But after a while, the tide started shifting. There were lesbians on TikTok, tonnes of them. It was as if they had their own secret club. There was nothing to that degree on Instagram. 'I wasn't expecting that for some reason, I was pleasantly surprised,' she says. 'It's a very close-knit community and I think we're all so happy to be gay and talking about it and that makes everybody else happy to be gay and . . .' She trails off. '. . . it's a great place.'

Cole is a lot shyer on the phone than in her TikTok videos. She speaks to me in the way you speak to a schoolteacher fishing for classroom gossip, polite and glossed over. But she's open when it comes to why she posts. For Cole and others, it's not just the fact that a lot of gay and bi teens are also on TikTok. It's more that everyone treats their sexuality as a positive thing, something to make relatable posts and in-jokes about. 'Because of how positively we talk about it on TikTok – being gay and being lesbian – that's definitely good for me. It makes me feel happy.'

India, a nineteen-year-old I come across on TikTok, has the words 'sad British queer kid' and a rainbow flag in her bio. She has bouncy, violet ringlets – almost like a cartoon – and thick, clear-lensed glasses. She only joined TikTok a month or two before we speak, but already has around 30,000 followers, most of whom are other queer teens. That's the thing about TikTok – it takes no time at all to become immersed. 'There are so many British LGBT people on there and we'll chat together and live stream together. I've made new connections through TikTok,' she tells me. India's videos are a mixture of mental health, queer and gender-related content alongside funny clips of her and her mates. One video shows her in a rainbow knit jumper dancing to lyrics from a PnB Rock song: 'I like girls who like girls'. The text overlay reads: 'Me trying to explain to my straight female friends that I don't fancy them'. She wouldn't have been able to make a video like that a few years ago, but TikTok has made her more comfortable in being open and out. 'I think seeing other queer people normalised things for me,' she says. 'I had a lot of internalised homophobia growing up, I think. Seeing that other people can be successful and be accepted helped me come out.'

Sybil, over in Denver, came out when she was thirteen. Now twenty, she wears her reddish hair short and tousled, with two nose piercings, and has the kind of chiselled good looks and straightforward eye contact that boy bands consistently try to recreate. She makes a lot of wry, funny talk-to-the-camera videos. In some of them she roasts tops and bottoms (she herself identifies as a top), in some she lip-syncs to music, but in a lot of them she educates her followers on the minutiae of lesbian life, urging them to be considerate. 'Friendly reminder that if you always expect butch women to be strong and "wear the pants" in the relationship, then not only are enforcing heteronormative ideas but you're also enforcing toxic masculinity, not only in general, but also on LGBTQ+ women based on how they look, and that's not great', she says in one of her videos, to the tune of over 30,000 likes. *PREACH*, reads one comment, from a follower who looks about twelve. *DAMN RIGHT*, reads another. *And that's the gospel truth.*

TikTok's lesbian community latched onto Sybil's videos early on for these reasons. Now she has over 700,000 followers after just a handful of months, a number that is 'growing comfortably'. Because she came out so young, and because she grew up in the very small town of Yelm, Washington – both of which forced her to become 'accustomed' to her sexuality 'very quickly' – she says she was already secure in her sexuality before joining TikTok. For her, it's more about being mindful of younger queers, those who might be in difficult positions that she was in years ago. 'Instead of making me comfortable in my own sexuality, it gave me the confidence to want to make others comfortable in their sexuality.' There's a give and take element to lesbian TikTok. A constant back and forth of absorbing and educating.

Sybil tells me that – out of all the online platforms right now – TikTok has the most solid lesbian and bi community. She notices it mainly when hosting and watching live streams; how they draw in the same followers, time after time, just like you might see the same faces in a queer club. 'You see the same people come back to a creative community where they feel safe with each other,' she says. 'Also of course the TikTok algorithm pushes the queer community together in that sense as well. So I'd say it's a pretty tight queer community through our own will to connect, as well as through the algorithm showing us other queer creators.'

§

For as long as the internet has existed, queer people have been using it to create safe virtual spaces. Some have even claimed that the internet itself is inherently queer; it has a queer sensibility built into its very framework. 'For one thing, there's the disembodied performativity of cyberspace, where no one knows you're a dog or whatever you choose to present yourself as,' writes David. J Phillips in the foreword of *Queer Online: Media Technology and Sexuality*. 'Queer folk are past masters at this game, as nearly every one of us went through the training programme during childhood. Even if we weren't singled out for special (unwelcome) attention as sissies, tomboys or other gender nonconformists, most of us survived society's sexual bootcamp – high school – either by masquerading and passing or living in the margins.'

It's true, especially when I think back to the earlier days of 'being online'. For those who remember the internet before the mid-2000s – back when you had to wait for your mum to get off the house phone so you could access the dial-up connection via a chunky grey computer – the internet felt anonymous, secret, hidden and, by extension, as if you could be anyone. A boy presenting as a girl. A girl presenting as a boy. A mysterious stranger with an obscure MSN screen name *tap, tap, tapping* indie lyrics to the girl they could never pluck up the courage to speak to in class. Identity was subject to change, malleable. Technology writer Joanne McNeil puts it brilliantly in her 2020 book *Lurking*: 'Early internet users made a choice to present themselves on three spectrums: private or public, anonymous or named, factual or make-believe. The extent to which one's identity mimicked real life did not have much bearing on the depth of one's online experience.'

It's not as if that sense of anonymity and malleability has disappeared entirely – although in the era of widespread surveillance capitalism and our increasing awareness of it, some would argue it has. Underground communities still proliferate in the internet's farthest corners. Secret burner accounts still exist alongside 'mains'. Anonymous Twitter users with eggs for profile pictures spew hateful words to those they wouldn't dare glance at face-to-face. But our online selves are now expected to be more like extensions or upgrades of our real selves. Our URL lives bleed into our IRL lives. Social media has, in some ways, become less about exploring hidden desires and the dynamism of our identities, and more a method by which to project aspirational, polished, public-facing versions of who we 'should' be. Where we once might have used the internet to escape the bright glare of outside society, the internet now exists within that glare, measuring everything from our social ranking to our employability, personal brand and trustworthiness.

Still, even as that shift came into being, the internet still offered opportunities to explore certain parts of yourself that you couldn't in the outside world – and as platforms like TikTok demonstrate, it still does. For queer people in particular that has often meant two things: the freedom and safety to be a more authentic version of yourself in a space free from judgement or immediate danger. And meeting other queer people who are doing the same, queer people who you might not otherwise come into contact with in your small town or social circle, maybe those you have more in common with, maybe those who aren't out other than when they're interacting online.

Like a lot of people now in their mid-twenties to early thirties, my earliest experience of exploring my identity online was through MySpace, which was having a major moment in the mid-2000s. Back then, I was far from recognising myself as queer – and even further from discovering any kind of queer community online – and yet MySpace offered an opportunity to explore selfhood and community in a more general sense, like a prototype for what was to come later.

For a lot of queer teens though, MySpace will have been their first example of what an inclusive online space could look like. Bisexuality was especially visible on the platform, in part because the emo subculture ushered in the idea that bisexuality could be 'cool', and MySpace was where the emo kids gathered (a quick scroll through Urban Dictionary entries from 2005 and 2006 reveals endless definitions of 'emosexual', loosely meaning 'any emo who is bi'). On MySpace, bi teens posted pics of them making out with the same gender, created bi groups to connect with other bi teens online and worshipped at the altars of bi musicians like Brendon Urie and Peter Wentz. While a lot of this bi visibility appeared to be aesthetic-based – more to do with optics than activism – it also offered young queer teens room to be themselves, which in itself can be viewed as political. 'Bisexuality – performative or not – was inherent to Myspace culture,' remembers journalist Hannah Ewens in a 2018 piece for *VICE*. 'If you weren't watching musicians smush tongues onstage despite having girlfriends, or a girl with a side-fringe touching boobs at a house party, were you even emo?'

In essence, the framework that MySpace (and social media platforms like it and before it: Bebo, Friendster, Faceparty) offered was a blueprint for a new kind of personal freedom; you didn't have to be who you were *out there* or only interact with the people *out there*. You could carve a new way. And, like the perfect conditions within a Petri dish, this in turn allowed queer communities to flourish.

It wasn't just social media that ushered in this brave new virtual world. It was blogs too – social media's weird, supposedly more intellectual cousin. As McNeil puts it, there were many 'bloglike things before blogs, like online diaries, web pages of notes and links marked with time stamps, zines printed at Kinko's and the novel-length walls of text posts that people published on forums and Usenet.' But after the advent of sites like LiveJournal, Indymedia and MetaFilter, all founded in 1999, the blog became a thing in itself, kind of like social media but not quite. Communities were cultivated in comment sections and following lists. Connections formed around the words and images that a user posted, rather than necessarily the user themselves. Your feed was a changing, mutable thing – a conveyor belt of content – an aspect that would bleed into social media platforms, like Instagram, later. 'Blogs and social networks were not only distinct but complementary, additive rather than rivalrous,' McNeil says of these early noughties blog years.

In 2006, at a time when a lot of us were busy HTMLing flashing GIFs onto our MySpace profiles, or else changing our Bebo skin to something more gothy or blingy for the third time that week, a twenty-year-old tech nerd from New York called David Karp was busy developing his own microblogging site. By then, Karp had been developing websites for years. At twelve, he'd taught himself to code. At fourteen, he'd started interning for animation producer Fred Seibert. By fifteen, he'd dropped out of school and at seventeen, he was working for the online parenting forum UrbanBaby, which was sold to the media company CNET in 2006, leaving him with a handful of money from shares. It was around this time that, alongside his friend and business partner Marco Arment, Karp began work on his microblogging site – which he christened 'Tumblr' – from the bedroom of his mum's apartment. Tumblr launched in February 2007 and within a fortnight the service had amassed 75,000 users. By 2010, it hit one billion blog posts.

Tumblr could have become anything. It was just a website built for short-form blogs and following other users. But something about it – the clean, accessible interface, the lack of Facebook-style uniformity, the pleasing fonts and rebloggable images – attracted a certain type of person, and then some more. Young people who were into fashion and subculture. Creatives who were into the plain, gallery-style look of the site. Writers who were into fanfiction. Misfits yearning for an escape outside of their family homes in the suburbs. And somewhere amid all of this, the site attracted swathes of LGBTQ people. Out of all the social media platforms and blog sites of the time – WordPress, Blogspot, Facebook, Twitter, whatever else – Tumblr, it seemed, was where the queer kids congregated.

It made sense: rewind to the Tumblr of 2010 to 2013 – the 'golden years' – and theories about queerness, feminism and social justice existed alongside GIFs from *The Virgin Suicides* and John Waters film stills. Self-styled digital queer nudes lived beside eighties sci-fi posters and nineties disposables of Chloë Sevigny. Webcam selfies of non-typical female bodies next to Audre Lorde quotes and reblogged excerpts of lesbian fanfiction about Kristen Stewart. Tumblr became a space that was neither academic – and therefore dense, inaccessible – nor rigid and heteronormative. Tumblr had a visual philosophy. The only currency was style and aesthetic or imagination, with marginalised communities representing their skills, interests and desires in place of the mainstream media often refusing to.

At the time and in later years, certain aspects of Tumblr were criticised for being vapid and apolitical. What use are a few pink-tinged digital photographs of some random white girl's pubic hair? What about real disruptive activism on the streets? How does any of this help any real cause? But while the inclusivity and usefulness of what was dubbed 'Tumblr Feminism' was rightly and fairly critiqued, there's no denying that the platform also acted as a significant intersectional space. To say otherwise would be to ignore the sheer breadth of communities that lived on Tumblr during that era. 'Tumblr has emerged in recent years as a chief locus of queer-of-colour political expression,' wrote digital anthropologist Alex Cho in 2015. Young queer and gender nonconforming people from all over the world were connecting and expressing themselves on their own terms through art, writing, fashion. This was arguably something that hadn't been done online before on such a scale.

Jender Anomie is twenty eight years old with bright, almost neon-yellow hair and a knack for wild, maximalist make-up. They're a friend of many friends, but aside from that I know them through TikTok, Instagram and Depop, where they showcase an endless series of vibrant, customised looks made from a flamboyant mishmash of vintage clothes and procured fabrics. Before all that though, there was Tumblr. That was where they connected with a part of themselves previously unseen, not just in terms of queerness and gender expression, but in relation to who they could be and who they wanted to hang out with.

'Tumblr was the first time I came across the kind of subcultures that I clicked with completely in a weird and frightening way. I know it sounds crazy, but before then it never really occurred to me that being a lesbian, for example, wasn't a bad thing? Never before in my life had I seen someone who was a normal person like me – not a famous person or something – that wasn't uncomfortable with the fact that other people were uncomfortable with them. Even things like girls with unshaven armpits were mind-blowing to me. And that shit has been around since forever, do you know what I mean? But I never connected myself with them until Tumblr. Tumblr blew the world open for me in that way. I felt like I was a casual observer of my life up until that point. And then it became: this is what I want.'

Jender paints Tumblr as a place which opened their eyes to freer modes of expression, an escape from their humdrum teen life in the drizzly UK town Bexhill-on-Sea. Other queer ex-Tumblr-users use similar descriptions. For twenty-five-year-old bisexual Huda, Tumblr made queerness seem cool rather than something shameful. 'When queer/bi/lesbian identity was being represented on the more fashion-y blogs – knowing that a model like Freja Beha Erichsen was bisexual, for example – it made it seem cooler, as opposed to weird,' she remembers. 'Tumblr also had a reputation for being quite NSFW and I think that kind of content really helped me explore my sexuality. It was kind of scary but also intriguing and I definitely think seeing that stuff as a teenager made me want to explore it in my sex life later down the line.'

Twenty-seven-year-old Wacera joined Tumblr ten years ago from Kenya, where she's still based. At first, she was into the curational aspect, how you could share and reblog photography and art. But it soon became a channel through which to explore her queerness. She dated people on there without ever meeting IRL, spoke to others whose experiences chimed with her own. 'It was like . . . "Ah, you can be out without being out of the house",' she laughs down the phone. 'It was like a library on there. You could find so many references. It was how I got to find out about butch girls and – I don't want to seem ignorant saying this – but all the different facets of being a lesbian. As in, it's not just lipstick babes, there's a huge range. I dated someone who was non-binary and it opened my life and my mind to that world. If I never got to be on that platform, maybe I'd be a little more ignorant or not as open-minded.'

Wacera gravitated towards Tumblr in particular because it wasn't this solely white, Western space – there were other queer people from Africa on there. 'Tumblr stood out because I could also see other people in the continent interact with this same LGBTQ content. It was like: it's fine, we're all together. They've vetted the content, so it's fine for me to continue, do you know what I mean? I'd be in chats with people from South Africa, Ghana, Kampala, and we'd be chatting about our queer experiences. We were just opening ourselves up. That was all through Tumblr.'

But the Tumblr dream died as quickly as it was born. By the mid-2010s, a vague version of the 'Tumblr aesthetic' – pastel colours, iPhone screens, cotton pants, armpit hair, a nostalgic sort of teenage joy and coolness – had been predictably co-opted by brands. Any irony or genuine politicism was flattened out into feminist slogan T-shirts and adverts used to sell products back to millennials in parallel with 'queerness' and 'feminism' becoming brand-friendly. 'Tumblr feminism quickly became marketable, its forerunners repackaged as new-age "it girls" for the Insta-generation,' wrote Ione Gamble for *Dazed* in 2016. If the platform had once been criticised for being 'vapid', now it was really start-ing to look it. The writing was on the wall: an aesthetic that had been built organically by communities of young girls and queer folk now seemed commercialised, dead-eyed, out of the times.

Of course, everything turns tacky eventually. But there were harder nails to be hammered into the coffin. By 2013, Yahoo! Inc had acquired Tumblr for an estimated 1.1 billion dollars. What followed was a drawn-out process of buying and selling and sloppily passing between hands. Telecommunications conglomerate Verizon Communications bought Yahoo! in 2017, and in 2019 they decided to sell Tumblr to Automattic for less than three million dollars. Amid all of this, the content policy became much stricter. Tumblr introduced an opt-in 'Safe Mode' in 2017, updating it to default in 2018, meaning that a lot of the adult content – NSFW illustrations, nudity, fetish art, the stuff that drew in so many Tumblr users to begin with – was hidden automatically. What had once been a space to express yourself artistically, sometimes graphically, without limits, had now become a vague incarnation of its former self. According to SimilarWeb, between December 2018 and March 2019 the site lost an estimated 30 per cent of its user traffic.

Queer users were especially impacted by the new adult content filtration system. In 2017, an AI glitch on the site meant that LGBTQ-based content was regularly identified as 'mature' and blocked from view (platforms like Instagram and Twitter would later also fall prey to this same AI 'glitch'). Tumblr apologised and attempted to rectify the situation, stressing that the site 'will always be a place where everyone is welcome and protected', but the damage had been done: Tumblr was no longer viewed as the queer mecca of the internet. It had gone beyond that. Even once the glitch had been fixed, queer users didn't exactly flock back in their droves. 'It's not like everyone was using it for porn,' one twenty-eight-year-old lesbian tells me. 'But the fact you couldn't have arty nudes or even queer erotica or illustrations meant it wasn't exactly conducive to exploring queer sexuality in a safe way or having a community around that. I guess it became boring, like your parents saying, "Yeah you can have a house party! But I'll be over there in the kitchen, watching you, and make sure you're in bed by midnight!"'

Like a lot of queers, I had long since migrated to Instagram by then, a similarly visual platform that had been picking up traction from ex-Tumblr users since around 2014. The fact I'd started using Tinder then too – an app that can be connected to your Instagram profile – meant that lesbian and bi people occasionally followed me and vice versa. On top of that, I regularly followed queers who posted content that I chimed with: queer illustrators, queer people in bands, queer writers, gay and bi folk with their never-ending carousel of mullets and homemade furniture and brand-new plants for me to smash the like button on and share and comment. They were all there; an echo chamber of my own design. A community of queers at my fingertips, very unlike that which could ever be experienced in real life.

Even then, though, Instagram was never a neat comparison to golden-years Tumblr. From the very beginning it had its own strict adult content restrictions and has regularly come under fire for its murky shadow-banning of anything 'sexually suggestive', with many claiming it disproportionately affects queer users, sex workers, racial minorities and those with non-normative bodies. In 2019 and 2020, the site's restrictions ramped up a notch. Accounts with OnlyFans links in their bios were being deleted left, right and centre. Users were getting reported for even mentioning sex in their stories. Queer-led accounts with photos of queer dancers or partygoers were seeing sharp dips in engagement – again, all thanks to an AI filtration system that judged what was or wasn't 'appropriate' to be shown on phone screens. If Tumblr had been like a strict parent, Instagram was like the sex-fearing moralising matron of platforms.

You could say that queer TikTok is the platform that properly filled the void that queer Tumblr left behind. It's become a newer, snappier iteration, a place for young lesbian and bi people to congregate and forge their own online communities. TikTok might not be as stylish, 'cool' or aesthetically pleasing as Tumblr was, but for a lot of young queers today, that's actually part of the draw. 'Gay Tumblr was a major space where I learned about my own identity as a bi woman, but gay TikTok feels much freer and also, honestly, way more fun,' wrote Rachel Charlene Lewis for *i-D* magazine in 2019. 'It's much more welcoming to be able to learn about your own queerness via quick songs and dances than it was in the era of thousands of people screaming at each other on Tumblr's internet about who does and doesn't get to be queer.'

I personally think that the evolution from Tumblr to TikTok is evocative of the specific times that we're living in. Back in 2011, we might have been satisfied with reblogging paparazzi shots of Winona Ryder or whatever, but queer kids today seem more interested in the here and now, in changing the course of the future, in current events and activism. Their use of social media is about being present rather than getting totally lost in nostalgia. And with its constant conveyor belt of straight-to-camera videos, TikTok lends itself to that 'right here, right now' feeling, both in how it's used and how it's consumed.

By the time this book is published, something else will likely be on the horizon. Some random app that is being formulated in Silicon Valley as I type, a mixture of everything that came beforehand. That's the nature of the internet – it's never static, never definitive, only ever understood in mysterious waves that crash and make way for new ones.

The internet might be transient, mutable, forever on the move, but so too are queer communities. We have always shaped ourselves to fit our surroundings – whether online or offline.

Shed old skins in order to inhabit new ones. Been pushed out of one space and had the resilience to adapt and carve out new ones.

'Queer theory perceives identity as fluid constructions rather than fixed notions of the self that may be "masked" or hidden behind smoke screens,' wrote queer theorist Chris Ashford in his 2009 paper 'Queer Theory, Cyber-ethnographies and Researching Online Sex Environments'. Such fluidity fits neatly into the nature of the internet and, by extension, the way queer people have always used it. We gravitate towards each other in one space, and then we move onto the next.

Either way, we always seem to find each other somehow. Even from our bedrooms, even when we're alone, even when there's nothing in front of us but a screen bathed in white light and our fingers, tugging, searching through the glass.

The internet has changed and shaped queer culture and communities beyond recognition. That much is certain. But if there's one aspect of our lives in which this change has been felt most prominently, most irreversibly, it's our romantic lives. It's dating.

CHAPTER EIGHT

Dating

It is sometime in 2016 – November, December? – and the air outside is ice-thin and glistening. Inside, where you are, the windows have fogged up, and now you can't see anything other than the shape of your girlfriend, moving through the dark. Up the garden path, key turning in the lock. Within the next two hours she will break up with you, but you already know this because of her WhatsApp messages beforehand, which were strange and distant. You try to steady your breath, mentally prepare somehow, but your skin feels electric hot. Everything is painful.

When it finally happens – her perched at the end of the bed, you in a hoodie with a cartoon on it – it is worse but also better than you thought. There is crying, possibly pleading on your end, although in future years your memory of what was said will disappear, like a face carefully cut out from a photograph ('Do bad memories delete themselves?' you will Google at 2 a.m., annoying yourself. The answer is yes, apparently). All you will remember is her mouth, moving. Her coat, zipped. The cat you bought together three or four years ago sprawled at her feet, disinterested. *So this is how it feels*, you think, *this is how everything feels*. Despair is a revelation.

Later, the two of you place a few toiletries in a bright blue IKEA bag-for-life and walk for seven minutes down the road to your flat, which you moved into three months before then, possibly in unconscious preparation for what was to come. You share a perfunctory hug goodbye, hair catching in your mouth, the air a little warmer. Then as soon as she disappears from view you scream so loudly you see white spots for a second, before leaning over and dry heaving into the grass.

The next few weeks go by like sludge. Mostly you spend them crouched in the bath, or else obsessively scrolling through badly formatted horoscope websites written by people with names like 'Cal' and 'June' who tell you that Jupiter is hurtling towards you and is about to change your life, or something. When you discover your ex has a new lover already – someone with colourful tattoos and self-affirming slogan pin badges – you spit your Super Noodles into the bin and message her, hands shaking, throat full of mucus. *Don't ever contact me again, don't speak to me, I am dead to you.* Or maybe you write something like *This feels weird LOL.* Again, the details delete themselves later. All you will remember are the two little ticks turning electric blue and the feeling: like your insides are being scooped out with a spoon.

In early spring your best friend helps you move back to east London. She plays t.A.T.u on the speakers and flings your clothes around the room. 'You don't need this,' she says, lifting up Harley-Davidson T-shirts and sweatshirts that smell like moth-balls. 'This is you from like 2008, not 2017,' she says, grabbing at American Apparel bodycon dresses and screwing them into tight little balls. 'Only bring stuff that makes you feel fuckable, *fuckable*; everything else must go.' In the Uber ride to Dalston the driver plays 'Crazy On You' by Heart and you cross the river on the 0:45 mark, just as the first cymbal crashes, cold sun glinting through the window. In the future you will hold onto that memory; it will remain clear like polished glass.

In Dalston a blue sadness lingers with you always – a heavy sickness, a dull disease. Everything looks painted in plain colours. Even when you are busying yourself with others – drinking whiskey with flatmates on the carpet, eating miniature tacos with colleagues outdoors, rays smoothing out their easy-going, open faces – it is as if you are reading lines from a boring play about somebody else with your name, living a life vaguely similar to yours. *I am sapping their energy*, you think, feeling your flatness stick to other people, watching them deflate. You want to shake them, show them interesting parts of your life from before, via a supercut. *See? This isn't me, this isn't me. This is an advert break.*

Then one day, a few months down the line, something gives. It feels quite sudden, an indefinable shift. You are listening to 'Heaven is a Place On Earth' by Belinda Carlisle on the way to work when it happens – the first glimmers of a new crush, or something to that effect. But the crush isn't focused on one person. It's about many people, maybe an imaginary person, you can't be sure. Either way, when you hear the purple-red guitar and eighties drums – *Oooh baby, do you know what that's worth/Oooh heaven is a place on earth* – you can feel your mouth opening, warm and tongue-thirsty, a flush that spreads. The only way to describe it is that it's like you have a crush poised and ready to land, arrow cocked back and waiting. *This is what it feels like to move on*, you think, *I am finally moving on.* You have never felt hornier in your life.

You take up smoking again. You start looking at yourself in the mirror, properly this time, like your eyes are cameras constantly recording. You no longer recoil from the gaze of others, as you did in the immediate aftermath of your break-up. You notice good things, like beaming sunlight and thick fudgy coffee and how you can sleep for hours stretched out on your stomach alone, dreaming. In future years you will remember this as one of the most joyful periods in your life. Lorde releases *Melodrama*. Britain makes noises about leaving the EU. A man downstairs is diagnosed with schizophrenia after posting cock rings through your front door. Everything feels bright and correct. 'When you wanna let go, when you wanna let go/When you wanna move on, move on,' sings Kevin Abstract on 'Runner' and you notice how your body is filling its skin now, how your face is actually changing.

Dating doesn't come easily at first. There are new rules to follow and you haven't had time to learn them. Before all this, you barely met anyone with intention – how could you? Tinder hadn't yet launched, nightlife was on the decline. She was your first proper, adult relationship. But now you must swipe through a carousel of 2D faces and decide which ones you'd like to see in 3D, drinking opposite you and talking about their jobs and exes and birth charts and the birth charts of their exes. The categories by which you judge people are arbitrary and detached: How long/short is their fringe? Are they boring or just alluringly aloof? Do they own those dogs in a 'lesbian' way or in an 'outdoorsy' way? You skip the latter. You also skip people on Harry Potter tours and white people holding Black children on gap years. You swipe right on girls who look bored, girls with DIY bobs and rolling eyes. Shauna puts it like this: 'You want someone who looks like they could be on ketamine, but they're not actually on ketamine.'

Queer Tinder is unusual. There has never been so much choice, you don't even have to leave your bed, propped up on a pillow, swiping – but still nothing remains anonymous. There are the same thirty people within a two-mile radius of your iPhone and some of them seem to be dating each other, others are friends. You know this because you look on their Instagrams and tagged photos and the Instagrams of those in their tagged photos and notice that you are now speaking to two, maybe three people in the same friendship group. Everything is close-knit and digitised; eyes are everywhere. Is this what it has to be like? *Is this the new way?*

You won't remember all the dates you go on, but some of them will stick. The girl with the hair like egg noodles who brings four other dates along with her and ignores you all. The sober girl with the soft grey dog and impressive plastic surgery. The girl who stays at your house for forty-eight hours, never touching, only speaking. The girl with two other girlfriends and one dangling cigarette, worn as an earring. The girl who invites you over to smoke weed while you watch the entire third series of *Girls*, in silence. The girl from San Francisco who wears a fabric thong ironically and sings Paramore with you in the park. The girl with the blue-dyed armpits who once spent two weeks at comedy camp or drama camp or somewhere she could sing. Later, you will meet the girl with the water-coloured eyes and the charity-shop leather trousers, the only one you'll end up falling in love with. The one who will eventually become your partner. Oh, *it's you*, you'll think when you see her. Everyone else falls away.

Before then though, it is rare for you to go on more than two, three or four dates (you only ever seem to oscillate between 'obsessed' and 'repulsed', as do they, through no fault of anyone's). But you will see most of these people again, somehow. In coffee shops, on the dancefloor at clubs. Strolling by your place with their new girlfriend and two whippet puppies. Having brunch with their exes, arguing down the phone at bus stops. And you will acknowledge each other on the street, like each other's posts on Instagram, orbit each other online like semi-distant planets. They will follow your life as you will follow theirs – a silent queer pact. And when you date new people, those new people will reference names that you know already, people you've dated, people who have dated other people you've dated, like an invisible thread drawing each of you together.

Soon you will notice that, since becoming single, most of your friends and acquaintances are other lesbian and bi people, and you will come to forget which ones you met in what capacity. The best friend whom your best friend met on Tinder. The girl who slept with someone you slept with and is now sleeping with another friend of yours. The person who used to date the girl who ghosted your friend for six weeks and the friends who you didn't know were exes but now it makes sense because why else would they be having so many intense and tearful chats in the smoking area.

'Queer dating', you learn during this specific time in your life, is not always about dating one person and then moving onto the next in quite the way you grew up believing it was for straight people. It sometimes turns out to not even be about dating at all. It can be about connection, the grey matter in between, platonic intimacy, or something else entirely. How did you all find each other? It's hard to tell. (In the first season of *The L Word*, this phenomenon is brilliantly satirised with the introduction of 'The Chart', a complex web written up by character Alice Pieszecki on a whiteboard, showing all the interconnected relationships and one-night stands that she knew of, both within her immediate friendships and beyond.)

Over the years, then, you come to understand queer dating as an invisible community among many invisible communities: tied together by transitory moments of desire and intimacy and friendships and fingers on glowing iPhone screens. But also by your queerness, and the unspoken awareness that queer folk often stick together one way or another. Not just because of likelihood and numbers – although that is a factor, especially in small towns, especially in times gone by – but because of community and understanding and a conjoined way of moving throughout the world.

In other words: when you find one queer person, you often find queerness in general, and then you find a whole universe.

§

Everyone agreed that 2012 would be an interesting year. According to various interpretations of the Mayan calendar, which ended on 21 December 2012, this was a year in which civilisation as we knew it would finally come to an end. Armchair astronomers predicted a sort of doomsday scenario based vicariously on the idea that the sun might align with the Milky Way, or else a mysterious planet would collide with the Earth and wipe out the human race (a notion that NASA had to repeatedly publicly denounce). Prior to this, a 2009 disaster movie titled *2012: Doomsday*, depicting a bunch of random, cataclysmic, earth-shattering events, grossed over $769 million worldwide at the box office.

As it turned out, 2012 came and went without an apocalypse – or at least no more so than usual. Queen Elizabeth II celebrated her Diamond Jubilee. Ecuador's Pinta Island tortoise became officially extinct. Vladimir Putin was elected as the president of Russia. Twenty-year-old Adam Lanza shot and killed twenty-six people at Sandy Hook elementary school in Newtown, Connecticut. And seven paintings worth around €50 million (including Picasso, Gauguin, Matisse, Freud and Monet) were stolen from the Kunsthal museum in the Netherlands, never to be found again.

One other thing happened in 2012 – although it didn't seem particularly remarkable at the time. A dating app called Tinder

– founded by Sean Rad, Jonathan Badeen, Justin Mateen, Joe Munoz, Dinesh Moorjani and Whitney Wolfe – launched within start-up incubator Hatch Labs in West Hollywood, California. At first it was limited to certain iPhone users and proved popular among college students. By the following year, it had expanded to Android phones and to more than 70 per cent of smartphones worldwide. And by the time 2014 came to an end, the app was processing more than a billion swipes, matching more than twelve million people globally, and was fast approaching fifty million active users. It had swiftly become the most popular dating app on the market and would only go on to get bigger.

Tinder wasn't the first dating app to succeed and it wouldn't be the last. Ironically, the most well-known dating apps before it originated in the LGBTQ community: Grindr launched in 2009 and Scruff in 2010, both of them helping gay and bi men connect by searching for other active users within a specific geographic radius. But as an app for other genders and sexualities, Tinder quickly picked up traction where others hadn't. Everyone could use it, and not just for hook-ups, but for relationships too. Furthermore, it was propped up by an idea that Grindr and Scruff had realised previously, and that older algorithm-based dating websites had not: that at the beginning of a relationship, all that really matters is looks. Mutual interests are a bonus, sure, but if you don't fancy them, you're not going to swipe right.

For straight people, the effects and after-effects of Tinder would be far-reaching and much discussed. But for queer women, they would be astronomical and culture-shifting in a different way (and I say 'women' in this instance because the situation has historically been distinct for a lot of non-binary people, many of whom have expressed frustration at the way dating apps are continually built around a gender binary). At a time when lesbian and bi nightlife was almost non-existent, and when social media was encouraging people to stay inside more than ever, Tinder felt like a simple answer to a complex maths problem. Suddenly, queer women weren't a rare and unattainable species, found only through a relay race of reading between the lines and being in the right place at the right time. They were there at the touch of a button, with ages, faces and geographical locations. If you wanted a drink that very same night with a real life lesbian or bi woman all you had to do was unlock your phone and find a willing participant.

To truly understand the impact that apps like Tinder had on the dating lives of queer women and by extension their communities and culture, we need to first rewind to right beforehand, to the 1990s and 2000s. This was a particularly weird time for queer dating. On the one hand, queer women had never been more accepted and less stigmatised. We had *The L Word*! Civil partnerships! Independent queer book shops! But on the other, it was still relatively difficult to meet one another, especially if you lived in more rural areas. There was online dating, sure, but even towards the mid to latter 2000s, platforms like eHarmony, OKCupid and Match.com still gave off the faint whiff of 'divorcee drinking wine alone'. If you weren't into clubbing or your small town didn't have one, your best bet was to become a sort of queer detective on high alert: *Are they queer? Do they fancy me? How do I know?* Straight people do this too, obviously – that initial guesswork is part of what makes dating fun for everyone. But for queer people, the pool is much smaller. Our spaces were (and are) harder to come by. And the room for error, the idea that you might read it wrong, held a lot more threat.

In a 1995 book entitled *Lesbian, Gay and Bisexual Identities Over the Lifespan: Psychological Perspectives*, professor Ritch C. Savin-Williams paints an especially bleak picture of the dating life of young queers in particular. 'Dating someone who is erotically attractive is seldom an option for gay male and lesbian youths,' he begins, doomily. 'The possibility of dating someone of the same sex is so remote that most youths never consider it a reasonable expectation. This separation of the erotic from the socially and emotionally acceptable (heterosexual dating) may produce self-doubt, anger, resentment and distortion in development during the adolescent years. If lesbian, bisexual and gay male youths have opportunities to explore their sexuality, it may be confined to sexual encounters, with either same- or other-sex individuals, which often lack romance, affection and intimacy.'

He goes on to describe the difficulties of dating same-sex partners during adolescence as 'monumental'. 'First is the difficulty of finding each other,' he writes. 'Most bisexual, gay male and lesbian youth are closeted – not out to themselves, let alone others. A second barrier is the consequences of same-sex dating, such as family and peer harassment, both verbal and physical. A third impediment is the lack of public recognition or celebration of those who are romantically involved with a member of the same gender. Youth learn that emotional intimacy should be achieved only with members of the other sex.'

In her 2002 book *Lesbian Love and Relationships*, Suzanna M. Rose takes a less foreboding approach when describing the dating habits of adult queer women during a time before apps. To her and her interviewees, queer women had full and thriving dating lives, but they didn't necessarily follow the same straightforward patterns as heterosexual dating (when dating women rather than men). Many of those she interviewed had friendships that developed into relationships, for instance, rather than 'traditional' dates, with clear-cut expectations and cinema trips and glowing introductions to parents. Out of those she interviewed, around 69–77 per cent believed that 'lesbian dating' was unique, citing aspects such as 'freedom from gender roles', 'heightened intimacy/friendship' and 'effects of prejudice'.

'Lesbians may find it difficult to discern if or when a friendship has moved "over the line" into a romance,' Rose concludes, adding: 'They also must create their own "markers" for transitions in their relationships, due to lack of access to public rituals of commitment such as engagement and marriage.'

Paula, forty-one, tells me that when she first started dating women in the mid-1990s, the most sure-fire way to meet anyone was in a gay club, the nights of which would be advertised on flyers or in magazines. Dating was a physical process, from start to finish, and you had to be active about it. When she moved to London from Washington DC at seventeen, for instance, she immediately bought a copy of *DIVA* magazine, spread it across her bed and studied the pages. There was a huge ad for the gay nightclub Heaven, and it read: 'DIVA DYKES GET IN FREE.'

'I ended up sleeping with a woman I met that very first night,' she remembers, laughing. 'And basically, in very lesbian fashion, moved into her flat in Finsbury Park and had sex for two weeks. This was prior to everyone having mobile phones, so I remember going to one of those old telecom BT phonebooths and going through twenty of these pay cards calling my best friend long-distance to tell her that I'd had sex with a woman for the first time and that it's changed my life! And she was like, "You've not even been there for a week".'

After that, Paula went clubbing all the time. Four to five nights a week, there were different lesbian and bi nights on in Angel, Brixton, Soho. You name it, she'd be there – often on her own to begin with, but she didn't mind. Mainly she went because it was the only way to meet other queer women back then, to be sure of what they wanted. 'You went to meet people to *have relation-ships with*, because that was the only way to meet people. Most people weren't out.'

'If I were to put a cycle on it, it'd be like: you were single, so you went to all the bars during the different nights of the week, catering to different groups,' she says. 'And then eventually you'd notice someone and maybe start talking to them, in a way that felt quite like school. And then you might hook up with someone right away or it might be after seeing them a number of times and finally talking to them. And then, well, you'd be dating. You'd stop going to nights because you were indoors all the time until you broke up and then suddenly you were back at the nights.'

After one long summer of repeating this ritual, Paula began to notice the same faces in the same clubs. A scene. 'It was a little bit like a soap opera,' she remembers. 'Especially in the smaller bars. After a while there would be an awareness of the different relationships people were having, and maybe you witnessed some fights and maybe you witnessed people getting together and sometimes the fights were really messy. There would be quite a lot of information about these people that you didn't know because you didn't live your life out in public. Your entire social life was really existing in those scenes. There was this strange public/private thing. For some people, the only way you could safely hit on someone or be sure that someone was queer was in those places. I wouldn't have known any other way to meet people.'

Juli, thirty-eight, recalls a similar experience. She moved to London from São Paulo in 2005 and, like Paula, spent the first few years going to queer nights alone. Again, dating was a physical, active process that took a certain degree of guts. 'I was discovering everything by myself,' she says. 'I've never had much problem going out alone, which helps. I'd discover clubs in magazines. I used to then pass in front of the club, but not be brave enough to go in. Then it took me a few times to be brave enough.' She went to G-A-Y Late in Soho a few times, although she didn't really like the music. 'I didn't like the places, I just went because I didn't have other options.'

Juli's wife, thirty-nine-year-old Katy, was never into clubbing. She'd moved to London from Colorado in 2009, and until then would mainly use internet dating sites like Match.com to meet women. But when the long-distance open relationship she was in at the time began to crumble, she started going out more and trying to meet women face-to-face. 'I started going out by myself because I didn't have many lesbian friends,' she says. 'Through that, I made friends with people in the clubs. Essentially what everyone else does in their teens and twenties, I did in my early thirties. Three to four nights a week, coming home at four in the morning, going to work.'

By the time she met Juli – in 2012, at a lesbian/bi night called Ruby Tuesdays in Soho's Ku Bar – Katy had perfected the art of knowing if another woman was interested. 'This is based on my own observations,' says Katy. 'You're in a club and first of all it's eye contact. You know the difference between "we accidentally met eyes" and "eye contact". And then there has to be a conversation. Just, "Hi, how are you?" – it doesn't have to be deep and meaningful. But there has to be an actual acknowledgement. You can't go up to a woman and start grinding on her. Then if you can get them to talk to you, and if you can get them to dance with you, then you can make out and then . . . the world is your oyster. Then you move in . . .' She laughs.

Dr Amy Tooth Murphy, an oral historian specialising in LGBT and queer oral history, tells me that this active, physical process of queer dating – revolving heavily around queer bars – dates way back to the 1950s and 1960s, to post-war Britain. 'The queer scene, for good or for ill, has always been based around bar culture,' she says. 'There are lots of historical reasons for that. Partly, it's about finding subcultural spaces where queer people can actually meet. And it's also about secrecy and privacy. So that bar structure is really at the heart of queer life.'

It's weird, then, to realise, that up until the 2010s the queer dating habits of women hadn't really changed for decades. The politics had moved forward, ideas about identity had progressed, assumptions about gender and sexuality had become less rigid. But the culture itself was based on the same few fundamental tenets: that queer women were hard to come by, and if you wanted to actively find them, you had to immerse yourself in a culture and make yourself part of a network.

§

In a UK government survey from the Office of National Statistics, it was found that, in 2018, just 2 per cent of women in the UK identified as either lesbian, gay or bisexual. Out of those 2 per cent, those in London were more likely to identify as LGB (2.8 per cent) over other regions in England, while those in the North East had the lowest proportion in comparison (1.8 per cent).

While these numbers might not accurately tell us exactly how many LGB women exist (they probably tell us more about who's comfortable revealing their sexuality for a nation-wide survey), the percentage of 'out' lesbian and bi women still feels shockingly low. For context: The percentage of millionaires in Britain is higher than 2 per cent. There are more people in Britain who think potatoes and parsnips grow on trees. And, most alarmingly, there are more people in Britain who think the Earth is flat. And while statistics can be shaky and subject to change, it's worth underlining what these numbers tell us: that if an LGB woman walks into a random bar to find another LGB woman, they are statistically more likely to find a flat-earther, or someone who thinks potato trees are real.

§

As a younger millennial, I am part of a very specific generation in relation to the internet. Like those older, I remember a time beforehand: I remember getting my first mobile phone, a chunky green-and-black-screened thing that could only be used for Snake and texting my mum. I remember the hiss and whirr of dial-up internet. And I remember boredom, *pure mindless boredom*, stretched out and silent and blank before me, quenched only by leaving the house and knocking on someone's door without warning them first.

However, unlike older generations, millennials came of age alongside the internet. We understood what being online could mean intuitively in a way that our parents and grandparents didn't (scrolling through dodgy torrents on LimeWire, coding 'Ask Me Anything' buttons onto our Tumblr pages). We settled comfortably into a digital future, rather than romanticising an analogue past. Yet we could still remember a time before any of it. A time before you could look at your screen, see which faces made you the most horny and proposition them within seconds. Even as a digital native, the idea of dating apps can feel weird to me. Like a supermarket, but for sexual conquests.

For younger generations, pre-internet, pre-smartphone memories exist only on films and TV shows and via word of mouth. Gen Z don't straddle both worlds in the way older generations do. To them, dating apps aren't that weird. What's weirder is the idea of going out to a bar with the sole intention of hooking up with someone without arranging to meet beforehand (one teen lesbian I spoke to described it as 'creepy . . . like hunting'). For young lesbian and bi people specifically, the idea of building a romance outside of those internet spaces is something that harks back to the past. And that makes sense: it's hard to meet other queer people. Why not just find someone you like online and build a romance from there?

Twenty-year-old lesbian Amy says she first started using dating apps when she was fourteen or fifteen (back when Tinder allowed under-18s to join the platform). Her dating life has always revolved around the internet. 'I guess before that I had queer friends online from Twitter and Tumblr,' she says. She met her current girlfriend through Tinder two years ago, but she's also met other queer people who are now her friends. 'I go to uni in Birmingham, which is quite a "straight" uni. So I've used Tinder to meet the queer people. I think a lot of people do that. I've met people in relationships who just have a Tinder to meet other queer women.'

Amy might occasionally go to LGBTQ clubs to dance or meet up with a date, but she wouldn't really use those spaces specifically to hook up or find someone to have a relationship with. 'If you're in a club you have to make all these assumptions about people's sexuality and interpret all these signals, which can be hard,' she says. 'And there aren't many queer women in gay clubs anyway, at least not in Manchester where I'm from. I think the internet gives you that assurance of someone's identity. You can feel a bit predatory going up to someone and being like, "Are you interested?" I think the internet is definitely preferable.'

Charlotte, twenty-one, tells me something similar. 'When I was probably sixteen, I'd meet queer friends via Tumblr and Twitter,' she says. Later, at nineteen, she started using dating apps like Her, Tinder and Hinge to meet girls. 'The primary way is definitely dating apps,' she says. 'I think there's an invisibility with queer women and queer female culture. All the LGBTQ clubs – that I know of anyway – are very much tailored towards gay men and setting up gay men and those are the only queer spaces that are mainstream and exist in an accessible way. There isn't that physical space where you can present yourself as a queer woman looking for another one.'

Charlotte describes the idea of approaching another woman in a bar or public space as 'so weird', as if the offline element infringes on someone's personal space. 'A lot of straight girls do go to gay clubs, so even in those spaces I'm like, "Are you . . .? Will you find it weird if I approach you?" So having it upfront, and already knowing if they're interested in women, or if they're queer, makes it a lot easier. You feel like you're going to embarrass yourself less.'

Twenty-three-year-old Megan, who is queer and non-binary, tells me that they've made out with girls or other non-binary people at parties, but the majority of people they meet in a romantic or sexual capacity is via apps. 'I can hook up with someone once at a party focused on non-binary people or queer women. But dating apps are pretty much the only way,' they say. As someone who has been in polyamorous relationships in the past, Megan says that also creates a double bind. It's hard to find someone who's queer and poly without using apps. 'Through Tinder, I had a poly relationship with someone who lives in the Outer Hebrides,' they say. 'In tiny places in Scotland and more regional areas, if you want to meet anyone into polyamory or anyone queer, you're going to find them on dating apps. That's literally the only way.'

§

Side by side, the dating habits of young lesbian and bi people can feel miles away from those even just ten years older. Post-digital culture is such a snowballing, ephemeral thing, and it moves at such a slick pace, that the world inhabited by queer teens today can feel like another universe to queer people of their parents' and grandparents' age; they were sneaking around and going to gay bars by themselves. Queer kids now are finding each other on TikTok, from their bedrooms, barely needing to move at all.

But if we take a step back and observe the whole picture, lesbian and bi dating culture hasn't changed that enormously – it just looks a bit different from this angle. As Dr Amy Tooth Murphy points out, before queer people had apps, we had personal ads – which would appear in traditional newspapers or else in 1980s/1990s lesbian erotica mags like *On Our Backs*. One more recent dating and social app – Lex, which launched in 2019 with the intention of connecting anyone other than cis men – is even directly based on such personal ads. Before it became an app, Lex existed as an Instagram account – @ Personals – that linked up queer women, trans and non-binary people via text-based bios. Anyone interested in the bio would then slide into @Personal's DMs, who would do the match-making. But even regular apps hark back to this old-school way of queer dating.

'It's not as if we've never had forms like this before, where people are basically putting their wares in the shop front,' Murphy explains. 'Personal ads have a really important place in queer culture – and again, did some of the work that straight people didn't have to do in their lives. Technically they can walk into a bar and meet people, but queer people couldn't always do that, especially if they were geographically isolated. So I think apps are just taking the place – with much more nuance and functionality – of something that has existed in queer culture for a very long time.'

There are other elements that haven't changed, either. Regardless of which generation you belong to, the same old stereotypes about lesbian/bi dating continue to persist. We're seen as knowing every other queer in our area and all their business (see again: The Chart from *The L Word*). We're seen as having overly intimate, almost co-dependent relationships that move incredibly quickly ('What does a lesbian bring to the second date? A U-Haul'). We're seen as remaining friends with all our exes, in a way that baffles our straight friends. And we're seen as falling in love with the wrong people at the wrong time, forever entangled in some sort of 'dyke drama' (see: any TV show centring lesbians, ever).

Murphy believes that these stereotypes can be understood from two separate angles. On the one hand, they reflect mainstream society's heterosexist view of both non-normative relationships (chaotic, deviant, messy) and women (hysterical, emotional, also messy). But on the other, a lot of queer women would be the first to admit that some of these stereotypes hold a glimmer of truth. Minorities (or 'a community of need') often turn to each other for more than just romantic support. They lean on each other for 'partnership, solidarity, safety and shared interests' in the absence of those needs being met elsewhere in straight society. Consider also the fact that our dating pools are smaller than cis, heterosexual people's, and it's no wonder our networks have been known to feel close, our relationships extra intimate, our platonic and romantic relationships blurred and complex – even if those queer dating associations can also be cartoonish, inaccurate, assumptive.

'When we talk about queer women's relationships there are a lot of stereotypes and jokes about how those relationships work,' Murphy explains. 'But Western women – in modern history – are supposed to do a lot of emotional intimacy work as well. So if we think about what we expect from women's friendships and then what we expect from romantic relationships, and we bring that together in a community where people often have even more investment, even more emotional energy, because of their own experiences of resistance, their experiences of oppression, it's not really that surprising when you look at the big picture that these relationships can get quite messy.'

The 'staying friends with your ex' trope arguably exists within this realm too. 'Queer people have historically gone through a lot with their partners, so to let go of that feels like a lot, right?' Murphy continues. 'Say you came out with your first partner . . . if you think about what coming out looks like, what you go through with that person . . . to walk away from that is to walk away from the becoming of yourself; your sexual or gender identity. So there's a lot wrapped up in it. It's interesting talking to straight people about this because they don't have to go through a lot of this. Their dating life exists much more separately to the rest of their life.' To queers, though, our dating life and non-dating life is often a little intertwined. And this isn't something that has changed: not in the 1950s and 1960s, not in the 1990s and 2000s, and not even right now.

It's been nearly a decade since Tinder first launched in 2012. Since then, the market has become saturated with other, more targeted or just generally preferable apps: Hinge, Bumble, Feeld, Lex, Raya. In a few years' time, those apps will become outdated and make way for new apps. And soon enough, there will be entirely new ways of meeting partners, technological and cultural avenues that haven't even been thought of yet, routes that will make the very concept of dating apps feel just as old-fashioned as a personal advertisement for a 'soft butch in my area' within the inky pages of a black-and-white newspaper.

Either way, queer people will always find other queer people. Where desire exists, so does a drive to pursue it. And where dating exists, a culture around it will always flourish.

CHAPTER NINE

Mental Health

TW: This chapter references self-harm, suicide, sexual abuse, eating disorders, depression, anxiety. Turn to page 209 to skip.

I t is the year 2011 – or is it 2012? – and you are staying at your friend's studio flat in Helsinki, Finland. You have been visiting for eight days, maybe nine, although it's hard to tell because the sun never fully rises in winter. Instead, the sky turns from grey-white to dark white to black, like shadows across a page in a book before it's closed. It is beautiful and bleak here. Snow spits out of the clouds continually.

You have spent most of the day alone because your friend works at a pharmaceutical factory on weekdays, just out of town, packing pills into boxes. She usually gets back around midnight. Outside there is a blizzard, so you remain slumped on her bed for hours, watching back-to-back episodes of *Desperate Housewives* and eating little Karelian pasties (*Karjalanpiirakat*), filled with rice and eggs. They are your favourites – your friend picked them up especially. But as you reach the third or fourth season of *Desperate Housewives*, they start to sit weirdly in your mouth, your stomach, your mind.

Soon, you can't concentrate on the laptop screen at all. The characters are yabbering now, nonsensical. Your heart is pounding heavily, erratically, like it does in the seconds before vomiting, and your face has become slick with sweat. What is happening? Have you caught a bug? Outside you can hear men's voices, rustling, but you don't know what they are saying – it's all in Finnish. And then a thought comes to you suddenly, like an envelope quickly pushed under a door: What if those men are trying to get inside the flat? They're right outside, after all. The thought seems objectively irrational somehow, but you hold your breath anyway. If they don't hear me, they won't know I'm in here.

The sweat-sick feeling won't go away but now it is tinged with this new paranoia; what if they break in here and sell me to human traffickers? You are realising now, in among all of these what ifs, that you sound as if you are losing your mind. People don't tend to think that human traffickers are plotting against them out of nowhere, do they? What sort of thoughts do most people have? But still you are glued to the bed with fear, your skin stretched tautly across your body. It is as if your mind has entered a new space, a dimension in which nothing feels clear or calm or correct. You wonder if you should ring someone. You wonder if you will have to go to hospital. Both thoughts make you feel worse.

Slowly, carefully, you crawl over to a pile of your friend's clothes on the floor and start folding each item methodically. You remember your aunt telling you once how she had felt like this a couple of times too. She would sit on the landing, matching pairs of socks together, arranging vests. Now you are doing the same thing. After an hour or two, maybe five, your heart gradually steadies. You stop worrying about the people outside so much. By the time your friend gets back, her flat is spotless, her clothes in neat little piles, colour-coordinated. 'Why are my clothes like this?' she asks in that straightforward Finnish way of hers, standing upright in the doorway. 'Have you been crying?' Your cheeks are wet. You hadn't even realised.

In London you look back on that time in Helsinki as an odd dream, a strange anomaly. But it will not be the last time you experience a panic attack, or anxious thoughts, or a flash of paranoia, or depression. In later years, at uni, you will sometimes be filled with such inexplicable anxiety that you think your brain might actually break. Depression usually comes afterwards, a post-anxiety crash. You will find it hard to get out of bed in the morning, find it hard to stop crying, find it hard to function. You will lose your appetite. You will drop to six stone. You will fuck up your relationships, behave in ways that make you cringe, behave in ways that make you scrunch your eyes shut and wish you could fold yourself up like paper.

When you are twenty-two or twenty-three, you will, for the first time, attempt to seek help. You will go to the GP and you will sob in a blue plastic chair and she will prescribe you 50mg of Sertraline, an SSRI, and you will wonder whether this little pill will be the answer to your prayers. It will not be, yet. In fact, if you had felt depressed beforehand, you now feel a little unhinged, definitively worse. Your mouth feels dry, your brain pendulous, swinging. You know you should persevere – 'Give it six weeks,' she said, 'you might feel worse before you feel better.' – but you can't even keep it up for two. You start to think that you are crazy – like, actually crazy. Look at that crazy lesbian, you think to yourself. You are the quintessential psycho dyke.

Later you return to the GP, thumb through the same Comic Sans leaflets, wait for your name to bleep red on the digital display. She prescribes you another antidepressant, Citalopram this time, 20mg. You ask to see a therapist, a counsellor, psychiatrist, anything at all. You are told to go on a website, apply online. Waiting could last six months or longer. Nine months to a year, she says, for 'talking therapy'. You take the printed piece of paper she gives you anyway, fold it up. The Citalopram doesn't work, it makes you feel spaced out, disconnected, separate from your body. The printout remains in your bag for months. It will take years before you see a therapist, years before you understand what 'therapy' even means, years before you understand the ways in which antidepressants can be useful.

Sometimes, in your darkest hours, you conclude that nothing can really help you. You think that this is your personality now (detached, moody, souring from within) and therefore it cannot be 'fixed'. But other times, deep down, you believe that the problem might not even be yours. You are told that poor mental health is partly genetic, that it is no different to any other disease, like Huntington's or alcoholism. But privately, shamefully, you wonder whether your body is trying to tell you something, whether your body is in fact screaming. Whether you are not a 'crazy lesbian' after all – whatever that means – but a person trying to break free.

§

For as long as I can remember, the 'crazy lesbian' trope has endured throughout pop culture. Even the phrase 'crazy lesbian' has a certain familiar ring to it. They are two words that hold hands, two words that seem to find each other constantly. If a woman is crazy, the trope implies, a lesbian is crazy times two.

This 'craziness' has appeared in multiple, overlapping iterations. There's the 'obsessive, unhinged' lesbian, prone to delusion and paranoia (see: *Black Swan*, both leads in *Mulholland Drive*, *Single White Female*). There's the 'jealous psycho' lesbian, usually driven completely insane by her unrequited love of an unsuspecting straight woman (think: Mrs Danvers in *Rebecca*, Eve in *All About Eve*.) Right at the top of the pyramid of course is the 'murderous lesbian', who we see time and time again in film and TV (see *takes a deep breath*: *Daughters of Darkness, Basic Instinct, Bound, Windows, Heavenly Creatures, Monster, Lesbian Vampire Killers, Lizzie, Women Who Kill*). These tropes are impossible to escape. Even one of my favourite TV comedies – Julia Davis's *Sally4Ever*, in which Davis plays the exciting and then frightening new girlfriend of the main character – feeds into the stereotype of the lesbian lover as demented, obsessive, a deranged figure who ultimately drives the main female protagonist back into the arms of a safe (read: heterosexual, male) lover.

Bisexuals are often portrayed similarly, though not completely. If the 'crazy lesbian' is driven insane by jealousy and delusion, the 'depraved bisexual' is usually a little more sociopathic. Think Margaret in *Liquid Sky*. Lisa in *Girl, Interrupted*. Jennifer in *Jennifer's Body*. Kimberly in *Pretty Persuasion*. Villanelle in *Killing Eve*. Chloe in *Chloe*. These characters don't care which genders they sleep with because they don't care about anything other than themselves. The 'depraved bisexual' will often use women as pawns in a wider game, or else just for the thrill of it. Crucially though, the 'depraved bisexual' is incapable of true love and inevitably fucks up the lives of other, more empathetic characters. They overlap with the 'murderous lesbian' sometimes for sure – although the bisexual is more likely to be driven to kill by boredom or for attention than passion (Chloe might profess her love for Catherine in *Chloe*, for instance, but she seems much more wrapped up in ruining her life).

These tropes have been around for decades – centuries in fact – and they haven't just existed on the screen. One of the first pieces of vampire fiction – *Carmilla*, written by Joseph Sheridan Le Fanu in 1872 – tells the tale of an evil sapphic vampire, obsessed with consuming young women. 'With gloating eyes she drew me to her, and her hot lips travelled along my cheek in kisses; and she would whisper, almost in sobs, "You are mine, you shall be mine, and you and I are one forever".' Elsewhere, in Djuna Barnes's 1937 novel *Nightwood*, same-sex love between women is described as an 'insane passion for unmitigated anguish', with the main character perceiving her own desires as 'something evil in me that loves evil and degradation'. In Susan Swan's seminal 1993 novel *The Wives of Bath*, one girl is driven so insane by her love of another girl that she murders a man, chops off his dick and sticks it to herself with glue.

It can be hard to pinpoint why these 'crazy queer' narratives persist, but they nearly always smack of homophobia and misogyny. They paint the queer woman as the 'other', as an entity to avoid and escape like a haunted house in favour of a safer, more family-orientated home. If straight relationships symbolise security and comfort in pop culture, queer relation-ships symbolise the antithesis: chaos, deviancy, occasionally even murder. In fact, what could better represent the danger queer women present to the status quo than a literal loss of life? The ultimate warning. The ultimate punishment. None of this is to say that writers and directors necessarily believe that queer women are insane or bloodthirsty – I'm sure many more recent writers and directors would be mortified by the idea. It's more that the stereotype has endured for so long that it's become embedded into how people write in their queer characters, embedded into how we consume them.

The 'psycho dyke' trope is so prevalent that it's long become a wry in-joke among queer women themselves. Like a lot of ridiculous stereotypes pertaining to queer people, it's one we've swivelled around and adopted. I've lost count of the number of stories my friends and I have shared about the 'crazy lesbians' in our past, the times in which we've behaved like 'crazy lesbians' ourselves. I remember a friend once telling me about two lesbians at high school who became so obsessed with each other that they refused to leave each other's side, even to use the toilet. They ended up using a crisp packet in the corner of their bedroom instead. I'm 80 per cent sure this story is total bullshit, but I just mean to say that the 'crazy lesbian' stereotype might have originated in pop culture, but it's trickled outside of that, become a myth within the queer community too.

Tropes like these can have a worrying knock-on effect when it comes to how we perceive ourselves and our relationships, particularly when it comes to mental health. In Carmen Maria Machado's phenomenal second novel, *In the Dream House*, she beautifully describes the ways in which this stereotype would hang, like an unwelcome apparition, over her comprehension of an abusive queer relationship: 'I am unaccountably haunted by the spectre of the lunatic lesbian. I did not want my lover to be dogged by mental illness or a personality disorder or rage issues. I did not want her to act with unflagging irrationality. I did not want her to be jealous or cruel. Years later, if I could say anything to her, I'd say, "For fuck's sake, stop making us look bad".'

For queer women with poor mental health, the trope can make us resent ourselves even further (if queerness is stigmatised and so is mental distress, what happens when we smush the two together?). Nobody wants to be seen as the 'psycho dyke' who's always 'starting drama', or the 'depraved bisexual' with substance or intimacy issues. Unlike the 'tortured male artist', the afore-mentioned aren't particularly romanticised. So often we might end up pushing against it. In a 2013 piece for the *New Statesman*, writer Eleanor Margolis explains how the trope actively prevented her from wanting to accept that she was depressed: 'The problem I now have is that I feel like a traitor for perpetuating the "crazy lesbian" stereotype. Every time I bring up my mental health, I can't help feeling that I'm letting the team down.'

Things get more complicated still when we throw in the fact that, simultaneously, many also view being a queer woman as an inherently utopian scenario (think of all the times you've heard a straight girl say that she wishes she was a lesbian because it would be 'so much easier', or the times queer people have viewed their relationships as a healthier or more functional alternative to toxic heteronormativity). Lesbians are supposed to be kind to each other. We're supposed to be good at communicating our feelings. Lesbians aren't supposed to lose their shit. We're not supposed to get emotionally ugly, or unhinged, or have delusions that human traffickers are plotting to kidnap us without evidence. When you are a 'crazy lesbian', then, it can feel as though you are losing from all sides. Perpetuating misinformed stereotypes while also disappointing those who might expect us to 'be better'.

Ironically – or perhaps logically, considering harmful stereotypes like the above – LGBTQ people do actually suffer from significantly higher rates of poor mental health in comparison to the general population. For queer women and also non-binary people in particular, the numbers are bleak. In a health report conducted by Stonewall in 2018, it was found that 79 per cent of non-binary people, 72 per cent of bisexual women and 60 per cent of lesbians said they had experienced anxiety in the past year. 70 per cent of non-binary people and 55 per cent of LGBTQ women said they had experienced depression in the past year. 24 per cent of non-binary people and 13 per cent of LGBTQ women had experienced an eating disorder in the past year. Across the board, these statistics also tend to be higher if you're Black, Asian or minority ethnic, differently abled or from a socio-economically deprived background.

It can be hard to wrap your mind around such numbers. Why might a queer woman, for instance, be at a higher risk for experiencing anxiety or depression than a cis, straight person? If this were the eighteenth century – or indeed as recent as the 1970s – it might have been believed that queer women were predisposed to mental health issues, because queerness was viewed as a mental health issue in and of itself. Although female homosexuality wasn't routinely criminalised in the UK in the same way as male homosexuality, it was still officially classified as a mental disorder ('sexual deviation') right up until 1973, when the American Psychiatric Association (APA) removed the diagnosis of 'homosexuality' from the second edition of its *Diagnostic and Statistical Manual of Mental Disorders* (DSM). Even then, it would take another two decades (decades!) for the World Health Organization to declassify homosexuality as a mental illness in its International Classification of Diseases (ICD). The implications of these classifications were loud and clear: queer women didn't just suffer from mental health problems; they were the mental health problem.

Of course, mainstream psychiatry has thankfully moved on since then. We know that being gay or bi or anything in between is no more a mental health problem than being left-handed or liking coriander. Instead, mental health figures among LGBTQ people can be recognised as a symptom of a much larger, more complicated societal issue – external rather than internal. LGBTQ people are more likely to experience hate crimes, discrimination and microaggressions, for example, while also being routinely failed when it comes to mental health services: all factors that can be understood within the bracket of 'minority stress' (a phrase coined by sociologists to describe the consistent internal strain of having to deal with the negative environmental and societal factors faced by minority groups). For people of colour, that minority stress often piles on two-fold (the Mental Health Foundation found in 2019, for example, that the risk of psychosis in Black Caribbean groups is estimated to be nearly seven times higher than that of the white population). The mental health outcomes of certain groups, then, are not so much about who makes up those groups and more about the ways in which they are treated.

To get a better understanding of how 'minority stress' might impact queer people, I rang up Nicole Treanor, Policy Officer at Stonewall. She stresses that queer people experience the world in different, overlapping ways, all of which can contribute to poor mental health. 'A queer woman at school who wants to cut her hair short might, for example, be bullied or called a discriminative slur like "dyke" – but then, simultaneous to that, they're experiencing misogyny,' she says. 'Another example is a Black bi woman who might not be "straight enough" for society but isn't deemed "gay enough" for the LGBTQ community, so is occupying those liminalities, which on top of that is compounded by racism. For queer women it comes back to the question of: "Where can I feel safe? What areas are for me? What spaces can I feel accepted?"'

Having it all written down like that makes it sound like all queer people are having a hellish time every second of every day and it's driving us all clinically insane! Of course that's not true. But the point that Nicole is making is that living in a heteronormative society as a queer person can feel discomforting on one end of the scale, and actively unsafe on the other. In a survey conducted by Stonewall in 2017, it was found that one in five LGBTQ people had experienced a hate crime or incident due to their sexual orientation and/or gender identity within the space of a year. Three in ten LGBTQ people tended to avoid certain streets because they didn't feel safe. More than a third of LGBTQ people said they didn't feel comfortable walking down the street while holding their partner's hand. And that's without going into all the instances of microaggressions that LGBTQ people experience on a day-to-day basis: people on the train gawping at you and your partner, someone at work saying they 'would never have been able to tell that you're [*whispers*] one of them', the way the word 'lesbian' sits awkwardly on people's tongues, if at all (think about it: how often have you heard a non-lesbian use the word without sneering?). These experiences don't bounce off, they tend to sink in (relatedly, Stonewall found that rates of depression are higher among LGBTQ people who have experienced a hate crime based on their sexual orientation and/or gender identity).

The numbers aren't getting better, either. This isn't to actively paint a depressing image, but simply to state the facts. In data released by the UK government in 2020, it was found that reported hate crimes towards LGBTQ people were actively on the rise. Between 2014/15 and 2018/19 the number of recorded hate crimes based on sexual orientation across England and Wales went up from 5,591 to 14,491 – a rise of 160 per cent. Again, writing these numbers down can feel dizzying, hard to pin to the same concrete reality in which we are told that LGBTQ rights are moving forward, that this isn't the 1970s anymore, that 'love is love' etc. But just because two women can get married now, or trans people can theoretically get gender affirming surgery, doesn't mean that queerphobia and transphobia have been magically eradicated. Hate crimes are still a threat to queer and trans bodies across the board. With that in mind, it makes sense that some might be feeling a bit . . . anxious, or paranoid.

Still, it can be hard to crunch the vivid complexity of the human experience down into numbers. There are real people behind these statistics. Yas, who is twenty-three and non-binary, tells me that they've suffered from mental health problems for as long as they can remember. They were a lonely kid, a depressed teenager, often feeling like they were on the outside peering in. 'I think people could tell that I was queer or gender nonconforming,' they say. 'Kids struggle with that. Adults don't give them that understanding. If anything, adults enforce that kids should be within these really rigid gender stereotypes, so when they see a kid that doesn't fit that so much, it's difficult for kids to process. It was difficult for me to process.'

Yas had always experienced hallucinations, which wasn't necessarily a problem in and of itself ('You know when you're a kid and see things and you hear things? That just never stopped for me.'). But in their teen years, the hallucinations became quite disturbing; they'd say hostile things, turned nasty, became harder to brush aside. 'There were some times where it got really dark and there were some times when I was self-harming and really suicidal,' they say. 'Especially when I was at college, I was really struggling with that.'

Eventually, at seventeen, Yas was referred to CAMHS (Child and Adolescent Mental Health Services), but the therapists they were paired with just didn't seem to get it. They didn't understand the complexities behind why they might have been struggling day-to-day as a queer person, but also as a British Turkish person, how those two identities might interact or brush against each other. 'I just felt like the people there were very out of touch with my reality. The woman that I saw was a quite posh white woman. Obviously, there's nothing wrong with that identity in and of itself, but I didn't really get the impression that she'd explored how somebody else's experience might be influenced by other intersectional identities.'

Yas says they've thought about queerness and mental health often, the ways in which queer people might be vulnerable.

'When you have trauma on top of trauma on top of trauma, and it's not one isolated incident – homophobia keeps happening or transphobia keeps happening, or a combination – then after a while that obviously has an impact on how you feel like you can exist in the world and through it. It's not something you can escape or get away from. I can never go out and have a day where everybody genders me correctly. That never really happens unless I just stay inside with one friend and hang out. I think that's why it impacts us so much.'

Existing in a society that values cis, heterosexual lives can be detrimental to a queer person's mental health. But, as Yas points out, the queer experience is not detrimental in and of itself. That is an important distinction. A lot of queer people I spoke to had been through traumas entirely unrelated to how society treats queer people. For many though, it was a lack of understanding among mental health workers surrounding what it means to be queer that ultimately hindered their recovery.

One twenty-six-year-old woman, Alex, told me how she'd been diagnosed with PTSD and BPD (post-traumatic stress and borderline personality disorder) after a series of traumas, including being raped while at university. She hadn't told anyone about the assault at first because she didn't want it to make her 'any more of a saddo'. 'I didn't want to be this sad person. So I didn't tell anyone for ages.' But after being flashed outside a supermarket a couple of years later, her body was triggered into panic mode, and she became intensely depressed, locking herself in her flat for a few weeks. Eventually she woke up at Lewisham hospital, before being sectioned. After that, she was repeatedly in and out of emergency services for, what she describes as, 'being nuts'. During one experience, she says, an emergency service worker asked her if she was a lesbian before she got raped, as if her sexual trauma and sexual orientation were somehow inseparable, as if it's ever possible to 'turn into' a lesbian. 'I was like . . . I can't be in this conversation; I need to go home.'

I've never met Alex, but I've seen pictures of her, with a mullet-cloud of ringlets and neon-powdered eye make-up, straight cigarette sitting between two fingers. She's from Liverpool, with a Scouse accent that dances down the phone like a melody, and she's quick with a dark, self-deprecating joke. But when speaking about how mainstream mental health services could do better when it comes to queerness, her voice becomes soft and thoughtful. 'I've always got the vibe that when I talk about my sexuality – especially in the context of therapy, when so much of my diagnosis and symptoms are related to sexual trauma – that it's easy for a straight person to connect the dots and think that I'm frightened of men and that's why I'm a lesbian,' she says. 'But it's not that at all. If anything, it made me live as a bisexual for longer because I thought it was less tragic to get raped as a woman that has sex with men, than it is for a lesbian, do you know what I mean?' She breathes in. 'I think it'd be nice to speak to someone that understood. I was born this gay, babe. If anything, it's a happy part of me. The one thing that my brain has done for me that's a good thing.'

Heather, a twenty-five-year-old genderfluid person from Halifax, told me that they first sought help for debilitating anxiety while at university. Their father had battled substance issues while they were a kid and, later on, they'd witnessed their mother die of cancer: two traumas that therapy can often help a person work through. But instead, sexuality and gender identity became the focus, rather than grief. 'I really opened up to [my therapist] about my mum and dad and childhood,' Heather remembers. 'Then I think it was the third time seeing her that I began speaking about a time I'd shared a bed with my brother and dad in a hostel. I think I was nine. And she went, "Do you think that affected you? Do you think that's one of the reasons you have gender issues and sleep with women?" I was so shocked by it. I couldn't believe she'd basically said I shagged women or hated my tits because of sharing a bed with my brother and dad. I think she also began asking if I'd been touched by them. I called my brother straight after and we laughed, but I still feel like what she said was wrong. He knew it too.'

Had Heather seen a queer therapist, they say, the experience might have been more helpful. 'They would not blame my gender identity or sexuality on my childhood. I think that's an old-fash-ioned homophobic thing to say. Like, "You're not born that way, you're made that way". It's a bullshit theory.'

It's clear that there's much to be done when it comes to navi-gating the mental health crisis among queer people. We live in a world in which lesbian and bisexual people are constantly portrayed as batshit insane on TV and in film and books, and yet we're simultaneously left by the wayside when it comes to our actual mental health, in real life. During my work as a journalist, I've spoken to quite a few mental health experts and mental health charities in the UK about how we can possibly turn a corner. Nearly all of them have pointed to the same obstacle: a lack of funding for UK mental health services in general. Without proper funding, we can't expect to make traction when it comes to training health workers in LGBTQ issues, or creating services specifically geared towards LGBTQ people's needs. 'If health-care workers cannot open up or learn and educate, then those services will not be effective,' says Miia Chambers, chair of Rainbow Mind, a mental health service for LGBTQ people across London and Manchester.

There's hope that the tide is changing. At the time of writing, the government has claimed to have injected around 4.2 million pounds into mental health and wellbeing charities like Samaritans, Young Minds and Bipolar UK. But still, there is very little information on how such funding might benefit queer people in particular. It's all well and good broadly investing in mental health services, but if those very same mental health services are routinely failing LGBTQ people, then the mental health statistics that I listed at the beginning of this chapter probably aren't going anywhere.

Most importantly though, mental health issues among queer and trans people will not disappear until queerphobia, biphobia, transphobia etc. disappears too, which will take more than a bit of funding and training. The dismantling, the representation, the attitude-shifting, will require mammoth work from the ground upwards. Nicole from Stonewall underlines that it's really important that people receive an LGBTQ-inclusive sex and relationships education from a young age in order to kickstart this process. 'It's a really important way to foster a culture of inclusion, develop more open and accepting attitudes from a young age and to tell young people that their identities are valid – including queer women – no matter what,' she says.

But also, education doesn't just begin at school. It also begins in how lesbian and bisexual people are represented in pop culture. These long-standing tropes – the crazy lesbian, the depraved bisexual, the psycho with the gender issues – hover above us like subtle spectres. They teach viewers and readers that queer people are off their rockers, that we have issues, that the root cause of any queer person's distress is probably their queerness or gender identity. This othering sinks into the psyche of queer people, and it sinks into the psyche of others, feeding into how we're treated on macro and micro levels. I'm not saying that we should never have murderous lesbians on screen (I'm personally quite into a lot of pop culture's psycho dykes; the scene where Chloe Sevigny walks down the stairs naked and brandishing an axe in *Lizzie* is nothing short of iconic), but that we should have as broad a range of queer characters as we do straight ones. There could be some non-murderous lesbians in a film, for example (imagine!). Or a bisexual who doesn't stab someone to death.

Outside of representation, down on the ground, lesbian and bi people need to be given space. Endless free space to be themselves. This is why it is so important that we preserve queer nightclubs, music venues, queer libraries, queer art groups and skate crews and safe online spaces. When we speak about the culture and communities of marginalised genders, we're speaking about something that actively contributes to our wellbeing. We're speaking about mental health. 'Moving forward, we simply need more affirming spaces for queer women,' says Nicole. 'Carving out spaces where queer women can feel safe, and where people who occupy all of those different intersections can feel included, will have a massive impact on their health and wellbeing.'

§

In later years, you begin to feel better. It happens slowly at first, imperceptibly. But one day your mornings are no longer punctuated with tears. Small hurts no longer incite outlandish reactions, for the most part. You rarely feel paranoid, or paralysed with anxiety, but when you do, you might see it approaching in the corner of your eye first. You might see it before it arrives – meaning you might then have a chance to stop it.

It can be hard to pinpoint how or why you turn this corner. Therapy definitely helps, when you are able to afford it and find the right person (who knew that verbalising your anxieties might actually lessen their impact?). As does growing up and growing into certain coping mechanisms. As does writing this book, to a certain degree. Other than that, you do not get into meditation or running podcasts or mindful eating. You do not escape the city and you do not get closer to nature or God or mushrooms or little crystals in a velvet bag. You do not do anything that you will look back on and definitively think, *Yes, it was that*. But you do come to stop viewing happiness as an end goal or single state. It is just like sadness: unexpected, hard to pin down, gone before you've had a chance to get used to it. Today you are happy. Tomorrow you might find yourself in the pits of despair. Feeling better is something you have to work on every day in minute and indeterminable ways.

If you could point to anything though, it is other lesbians who pull you through some of the worst bits. It is your friend arriving at yours at 9 p.m. with a bottle of Famous Grouse and dragging you to the nearest gay club. It is dancing to Ciara until the sky tints rose-gold and spinning around lamp posts on the way home. It is sunbathing topless in the garden with your housemates and the sunflowers bending behind you. It is the sticky heat of your girlfriend in the morning and it is your old friendships and your new friendships, and it is every day that you wake up feeling free and easy and as if there is nothing festering inside you.

Did you feel so wretched back then because you are queer? Of course not. People feel wretched when they are straight too. People feel wretched when they have the whole world laid out in front of them, a red carpet of their own design. But being queer means you are already part of a system that doesn't always seem to understand you. Mental health problems can exist through a lens of shame and isolation; anger gets magnified.

The queer experience never got you into this mess, but the queer experience was there to pull you out of it. You are still a crazy lesbian for sure – sometimes even a psycho dyke – but over the years you've come to realise that maybe that's not such a bad thing. It's not a good thing either. It just is.

THE FUTURE

It is 2015 and Grace Jones is sitting across from me in a south London restaurant. She's wearing a billowing leather cape, black aviator hat and, until moments ago, huge goggle-like sunglasses strapped around her head like machinery. There is a bottle of red wine and a pile of lamb chops in front of us, glistening in the near darkness. 'Thank you, darling, *thank you*,' she says to nobody and everyone at once, her accent a strange lilting mixture of Jamaican, Parisian, London and New York, the bases and intonations overlapping and blending into one melodic miasma. She cocks one eyebrow at me in recognition and I breathe in, transfixed.

I'm here to interview her for *Dazed*, where I have recently become music editor. They let me have this one, I think, because they know what a diehard Grace Jones fan I am. The first tattoo I ever got was her actual face on my leg – at age twenty-one on a whim – despite the fact I'm generally not a proponent of having somebody else's face tattooed on your entirely different body, but she's an exception. She's on my left calf, smoking a cigarette forever until I'm dead. In fact, she'll still be smoking the cigarette there when I *am* dead, technically, and I imagine she'll be the last of me to go, taking her final drag once my corpse eventually rots and slowly turns to mulch in the dirt.

Anyway, I do not show her the tattoo and I do not reveal any inkling of fanaticism. Instead, I try to rearrange my trousers so that she does not see herself seeing herself, in miniature. We cover a lot of ground over dinner: age, art, pop music, racism in the fashion industry, LSD and how it has given her a third eye, a sixth sense of awareness, a sensitivity to what is happening 360 degrees around her. 'I plugged into all of it,' she tells me, gesturing at the space in front and behind her, before pouring her red wine from two feet high so it splashes and swills into the glass below, creating a mini whirlpool.

Our conversation eventually turns to gender and sexuality. 'Only you know how you feel inside regardless of what name is put on it.' She shrugs, digging a knife into the last of her lamb chops. 'Some people are both genders. I think you just come out the way you come out and you have to embrace it, honestly. I sometimes feel very masculine. When I got married to Atila [Altaunbay] he used to say to my mum, "I married a man" because of my unfeminine ways. But that's how I feel. I feel feminine when I feel feminine. I feel masculine when I feel masculine. I am a role-switcher.'

She pauses for a moment, fork glinting in the air, before continuing, 'Hiding, secrets, and not being able to be yourself is one of the worst things ever for a person. It gives you low self-esteem. You never get to reach that peak in your life. You should always be able to be yourself, and be proud of yourself.'

Fluidity is something Grace Jones has spoken about for decades (hardly surprising coming from the artist whose most famous album cover, for *Nightclubbing*, is her in an angular tailored suit-jacket, bare chest matte and muscular, flat top rigid and close-cut). In 1985, when interviewed on the Australian current affairs programme *Day By Day*, she was asked, oddly and pointedly, if she was feminine or if she 'liked being masculine', as if any normal person should have to choose. 'I like being both actually,' she drawled back. 'It's not "being masculine", it's an attitude really. "Being masculine" – what is that? Can you tell me . . .? I think I just act the way I feel, and I've always felt a lot of the male of my family influencing me. I lived with males all my life, whether it was my father, or my grandfather or brothers and we all rub off on each other.'

The interviewer then butts in, hungry for a scoop: 'Does that carry through to your sexual preference?'

'Well that depends.'

'Do you find women attractive?' he digs.

'I find women attractive and I think if I didn't, I wouldn't find myself attractive. I think one has to begin first with themselves and then go from there. And for me to say I don't find women attractive would be saying that I don't find myself attractive.'

'Does that make you bisexual?' he tries again.

'It doesn't make me anything,' Grace counters. 'It's ridiculous trying to categorise people's feelings or saying, "What does one prefer?" There's no comparison. You can't just say one's better than the other or one's worse than the other, I prefer one to the other. It's just: do what you feel when you feel like it, if you feel like it.'

'That may to some people be quite shocking.'

'What's shocking? To do what you feel when you feel like it? If you feel like it? It's just—'

'I guess because people seem to categorise things,' he interrupts, floundering.

Grace adjusts her big black sunglasses. 'Do what you want,' she says. 'I do what I want. I don't put me in a category, and I don't make comparisons and I don't say I prefer one to this or one to that because that's like saying "I'll never do this and I'll never do that" and one really doesn't know, do they? If one is put into that situation, one really never knows what they're going to do. Would you eat a cockroach if you're hungry? You can't say, can you?'

'Do you like shocking people, can I ask you that?'

'Does *that* shock you?' she replies, faintly amused. They get into a back and forth about cockroaches. 'In some places, a cockroach might be a delicacy,' Grace breaks into a mischievous laugh then and glances off camera, as if to put a line underneath the conversation. The interviewer looks deflated.

Grace Jones might have confounded this particular interviewer in 1985, but her words fit neatly into the prevailing vibe among young people today, some thirty years later, many of whom are refusing to label themselves in the way their parents did. Where you might have once been expected to choose between 'straight', 'bisexual' or 'gay', younger generations aren't so bothered about attaching such fixed words onto feelings, which by their very nature can be complicated and fluctuating and subject to change.

This loosening of attitudes isn't just a stereotype (although it sounds like one: old people are obsessed with genitals! Young people are basically all one polyamorous gender!). In a 2018 study, it was found that Gen Z (those born between 1996 and 2010) are significantly more openly fluid when it comes to sexuality than previous generations. Just 66 per cent of Gen Z think of themselves as completely straight, compared to 71 per cent of millennials, 85 per cent of Gen X and 88 per cent of Baby Boomers (those born between 1946 and 1964). Among British school children, it was also found that 60 per cent of fifteen- to sixteen-year-olds think sexuality is a sliding scale and that it's possible to be anywhere in between.

This changing perception of identity being fluid, not attached to binary, extends to gender itself. Over half of Gen Z know someone who uses gender-neutral pronouns (they, them, ze). Seven in ten of Gen Z think it's important for public spaces to provide access to gender-neutral bathrooms, compared with 58 per cent of younger millennials and 56 per cent of older millennials. Gen Z were also found to be much less likely to buy products specifically geared towards their own gender in comparison to millennials. For a long time, gender has acted as a strict organising system, a way of separating behaviours and interests, but that system is now being dismantled. What *is* gender and sexuality anyway? None of us really know or agree. All we can do is try to go with what feels right, in our gut. This is what Grace Jones was getting at.

I thought a lot about fluidity while writing this book. What LGBTQ culture might look like in the future, as ideas about gender and identity become increasingly unfixed. Will 'queer culture' still exist if queerness becomes the norm, or will it just be 'culture'? What is the future of lesbian and bi communities when young people might no longer wish to prescribe to terms like 'lesbian' and 'bi' anyway? Do non-monosexual identities destabilise the gay histories and subcultures that came before them? Some older generations have expressed anxiety surrounding these questions. 'In the first decade or so after the Stonewall riots, gay people needed to send the clearest, loudest, most set-in-stone message about our sexuality and identity possible,' wrote gay critic Jim Farber for *Slate* magazine in 2019. 'The lack of nuance in our announcement eliminated any wiggle room for the benighted to dismiss our feelings as fad, provocation or illusion. Because we had been told, in countless ways, clear and implicit, that we don't exist, and certainly shouldn't, only the most strident and narrow counter argument would begin to make our point. More, it was the surest way to keep from getting shut back into the closet, at least in the minds of those who couldn't conceive of us existing anywhere else.'

I'm of the opinion that handwringing and fixating on the past has never done liberation nor culture any favours. Queer culture must be water, or else we are at risk of mimicking the heteronormative system that attempts to subjugate us based on arbitrary, abstract notions about how a person ought to be. Of course, it is human nature to attempt to put people into neat little boxes because it makes us feel stable and safe. For gay, lesbian and bi people, straightforward labels have also been empowering. A way of saying, 'This is what I am and you can't change me.' Back in the day, and even now, when proponents of conversion therapy have attempted to claim that sexual orientation is in fact *not fixed*, to say, 'I was born this way' is a means of hammering home that our identities are what we say they are. That our labels are as true and valid as those of straight people.

But sexual fluidity and gender nonconformity are not in opposition to lesbian, bi and gay identities – they are in tandem. The fight for gay rights paved the way for younger people to be able to express themselves in more authentic ways. Wherever you exist on the spectrum, the ultimate goal is surely to open the world up to all of us and to respect how people identify and wish to present. 'True queer liberation means that we believe everyone when they speak about and self-determine their sexuality – even in the vaguest of terms – whether or not they have the experience, public performance or "credentials" to underscore their identity,' wrote Otamere Guobadia for *Dazed* in 2019. 'We believe them because we have an obligation to do so. To deny them the words and agency to determine their sexuality is to deny it to all queer people.'

The future of lesbian and bi culture is just that: the future. It will be whatever young queers shape it to be, because it's theirs to shape. I wrote this book because I wanted to create a snapshot of what modern lesbian and bi culture looks like today and how it came to be. I wanted to glance at the past in order to understand the present – or as much as the 'present' exists when the world feels so fast-moving and fragmented and chaotic.

But the future is an unknown quantity. The clubs of the future will be nothing like the clubs I went to as a teenager. The films will be nothing like the ones we grew up watching. The TV shows, the style codes, the great cosmic expanse of the internet; all of these are changing at a rate quicker than at any point in history. I am excited to see how queer culture unfurls in front of us at the hands of young people, how the world might continue to open up, again and again; a sunflower lifting itself higher over a fence.

My dinner with Grace Jones has to end at some point, unfortunately. She has meetings, she says, even though it is 10 p.m. at night. But first we have shots of sambuca at the bar. At this point I'm nearly drunk but not quite. I've been there for ages (she was two hours late, which I am told was quite punctual).

We say our goodbyes and then she straightens up and surveys me for a second, like a dial trying to settle on a compass. After a moment she leans in to say something. At the time I thought what she said was a compliment. Half a decade later, I think she was dispensing a word of advice: 'I love to see a young female go get 'em.'

And then she's gone, cape swirling behind her, aviator hat flapping into the night.

ACKNOWLEDGEMENTS

Firstly, I would like to thank my mum for giving birth to me and for all the love you showered upon me from thereon afterwards. You are my favourite person, always.

I would also like to thank my brilliant agent, Hayley Steed, who made me believe in this book before it was even a proper concept. A huge thank you to the talented editors at Coronet – Hannah Black, Erika Koljonen and Natalie Young. Your enthusiasm and meticulousness throughout this entire process has been a constant delight and learning curve. A big thank you to my publicist Steven Cooper. Thank you also to Theis Anderson for your smart and sensitive interjections when it came to the manuscript. Thank you, Jo Kiely, for your photographic talents and friendship. And thank you Holly Ovenden for designing an incredible cover which looks like some kind of 1980s futuristic vaporwave situation.

Thank you to my Grandma, Grandpa, Lily, Jessica, Emily, Eleanor, Iris and Henry. You are all brilliant and strange and special and I love you all equally in wildly different ways.

Thank you to Shauna, my best mate and confidante, for

allowing me to mention you so often in print and online and in 85 per cent of anecdotes. I will never forget telling you I was writing this book, at 2AM, in a hot tub, and you were like "Cool. Want another tequila?" Thanks for keeping my feet on the ground and for always topping up my drink.

Thank you, goblins – a collective of brilliant writers and best friends – for reading this manuscript first and for your kind and razor-sharp suggestions throughout. You've all made me a better writer.

Thank you to old friends and new friends who have shaped and supported me along the way: Alexis, Nat, Melissa, Emma R, Kati, Hanne, Emma G, Lauren, Hannah, Sammi, Coco, Bella, Herbs. Also thank you Bill, Mand and Dinky (I will never forget how you let me write the majority of this book in your attic).

Thank you to all my colleagues at VICE UK and everyone at DAZED before them (shout out Sirin and Ione). Thank you, Owen Myers for giving me my first real writing job and for teaching me so much about writing and pop music.

Thank you to all the LGBTQ+ people who spoke to me for this book, and to the queer community at large. It has been a real delight and honour to have heard so many of your stories and ways of viewing the world. I have learned so much that I will keep with me, and that I hope readers of this book will keep with them too.

Thank you to The Joiners Arms, The George and Dragon, Dalston Superstore and all the dancefloors that raised me.

And thank you Alice. For all your support, and for everything we share together. I love you so much.

BIBLIOGRAPHY

'The Butch Woman Inside James Dean or 'What Kind of Person Do You Think a Girl Wants?" – Marie Cartier (Sexualities, Vol. 6 issue 3-4. SAGE journals; 2003)

Encyclopedia of Lesbian Histories and Cultures – Bonnie Zimmerman (Routledge; 2003)

'An Open Letter to Mary Daly' – Audre Lorde (1979)

'How to Bring Your Kids Up Gay' – Eve Kosofsky Sedgwick (*Social Text*, no. 29. Duke University Press; 1991)

Gender Trouble – Judith Butler (Routledge; 1990)

Fear of a Queer Planet – Michael Warner (*Social Text*, no. 29. Duke University Press; 1991)

Female Masculinity – Jack Halberstam (Duke University Press; 1998)

Want – Lynn Steger Strong (Henry Holt & Company; 2020)

'New Notes On Lesbianism' – Cheryl Clarke (1982)

Naked City: The Death and Life of Authentic Urban Places – Sharon Zukin (Oxford University Press; 2009)

There Goes the Gayborhood? – Amin Ghaziani (Princeton University Press; 2014)

'Lesbian Musicalities, Queer Strains and Celesbian Pop' – Jodie Taylor (*Redefining Mainstream Popular Music,* Routledge; 2013)

'Querying Sex, Gender, and Race through the Queercore Zine Movement' – Camille Erickson (*Gateway Prize for Excellent Writing,* Paper 4; 2013)

Gender, Branding, and The Modern Music Industry – Kristin Lieb (Routledge; 2013)

Lesbian Cinema After Queer Theory – Dr Clara Bradbury-Rance (Edinburgh University Press; 2019)

'Skirting the Issue: Lesbian Fashion for the 1990s' – Inge Blackman and Kathryn Perry (*Feminist Review*, no. 34. Sage Publications; 1990)

'Lesbian Aesthetics, Aestheticizing Lesbianism' – Karen Tongson (*Nineteenth Century Literature*, Vol. 60, issue 3. University of California Press; 2005)

Deviations – Gayle Rubin (Duke University Press; 2012)

Zami: A New Spelling Of My Name – Audre Lorde (Persephone Press; 1982)

Queer Online: Media Technology & Sexuality – David J. Phillips (*Digital Formations*, Vol 40; 2007)

Lurking – Joanne McNeil (Picador; 2020)

'Sensuous Participation: Queer Youth of Color, Affect, and Social Media' – Alexander Cho (University of Texas at Austin; 2015)

'Queer Theory, Cyber-ethnographies and Researching Online Sex Environments' – Chris Ashford (*Information & Communications Technology Law*, Vol. 18, no. 3; 2009)

'Lesbian, Gay Male, and Bisexual Adolescents' – Ritch C. Savin-Williams (*Lesbian, Gay and Bisexual Identities Over the Lifespan: Psychological Perspectives.* Oxford University Press; 1995)

Lesbian Love and Relationships – Suzanna M. Rose (Routledge; 2002)

Carmilla – Sheridan Le Fanu (1872)

Nightwood – Djuna Barnes (Faber and Faber; 1936)

The Wives of Bath – Susan Swan (Granta; 1993)

In the Dream House – Carmen Maria Machado (Profile; 2019)

FURTHER READING LIST

The Price of Salt – Patricia Highsmith (Coward-McCann; 1952)
Rubyfruit Jungle – Rita Mae Brown (VT: Daughters; 1972)
The Faggots & Their Friends Between Revolutions – Larry Mitchell (Calamus Press; 1977)
The Color Purple – Alice Walker (Harcourt Brace Jovanovich; 1982)
Zami: A New Spelling of My Name – Audre Lorde (Persephone Press; 1982)
Sister Outsider – Audre Lorde (Crossing Press; 1984)
Oranges Are Not the Only Fruit – Jeanette Winterson (Pandora Press; 1985)
Gender Trouble – Judith Butler (Routledge; 1990)
How to Bring Your Kids Up Gay – Eve Kosofsky Sedgwick (Social Text, no. 29. Duke University Press 1991)
Stone Butch Blues – Leslie Feinberg (Firebrand Books; 1993)
Fear of a Queer Planet – Michael Warner (*Social Text*, no. 29. Duke University Press; 1993)
Female Masculinity – Jack Halberstam (Duke University Press; 1998)
Tipping the Velvet – Sarah Waters (Virago; 1999)
Exile and Pride: Disability, Queerness, and Liberation – Eli Clare (Duke University Press; 1999)
The Queer Art of Failure – Jack Halberstam (Duke University Press; 2011)
Gender Failure – Ivan E. Coyote and Rae Spoon (Arsenal Pulp Press; 2014)

Under the Udala Trees – Chinelo Okparanta (Houghton Mifflin; 2015)

The Argonauts – Maggie Nelson (Graywold Press; 2015)

Trans* – Jack Halberstam (University of California Press; 2017)

Born Both: An Intersex Life – Hida Viloria (Hachette US; 2017)

Paul Takes the Form of a Mortal Girl – Andrea Lawlor (Rescue Press; 2017)

Queer Sex: A Trans and Non-Binary Guide to Intimacy, Pleasure and Relationships – Juno Roche (Jessica Kingsley Publishers; 2018)

Her Body and Other Parties – Carmen Maria Machado (Graywold Press; 2017)

In the Dream House – Carmen Maria Machado (Profile; 2019)

The Stonewall Reader – Jason Baumann and Edmund White (Penguin Classics; 2019)

On Earth We're Briefly Gorgeous – Ocean Vuong (Jonathan Cape; 2019)

We Have Always Been Here: A Queer Muslim Memoir – Samra Habib (riverrun; 2019)

HoodWitch – Faylita Hicks (University of Chicago Press; 2019)

Queer Intentions – Amelia Abraham (Picador; 2019)

Diary Of a Drag Queen – Crystal Rasmussen (Ebury; 2019)

Unicorn: The Memoir of a Muslim Drag Queen – Amrou Al-Kadhi (4th Estate; 2019)

Sissy: A Coming-of-Gender Story – Jacob Tobia (G.P. Putnam's Sons; 2019)

Real Life – Brandon Taylor (Daunt Books; 2020)

All My Mother's Lovers: A Novel – Ilana Masad (Penguin Random House USA; 2020)

Romance in Marseille – Claude McKay (Penguin Classics; 2020)

Something That May Shock and Discredit You – Daniel M. Lavery (Atria Books; 2020)

In Their Shoes: Navigating Non-Binary Life – Jamie Windust (Jessica Kingsley Publishers; 2020)

What it Feels Like For a Girl – Paris Lees (Particular Books; 2020)

Felix Ever After – Kacen Callender (Balzer + Bray; 2020)

Growing Older as a Trans And / Or Non-Binary Person – Jennie Kermode (Jessica Kingsley Publishers; 2021)

Detransition, Baby: A Novel – Torrey Peters (Profile Books; 2021)

Transitional – Munroe Burgdorf (Bloomsbury; 2022)

The Transgender Issue – Shon Faye (Allen Lane; 2021)

LGBTQ+ UK CHARITIES AND ORGANISATIONS

Stonewall
LGBT Foundation (LGBTQ+ mental health and wellbeing)
MindOut (LGBTQ+ mental health and wellbeing)
Centered (LGBTQ+ organisation focussed on diversity)
Ask (LGBTQ+ youth homelessness charity)
Galop (LGBTQ+ anti-violence charity)
Birmingham LBGT (LGBTQ+ mental health and community building)
Gendered Intelligence (Trans-led, trans-involved grassroots organisation focussed on awareness, community building and wellbeing)
Black Trans Alliance (Black-led organisation supporting Black trans people in London)
London Gaymers (A safe place for London's LGBTQ+ gaming community)
Manchester Pride (Opportunity building for LGBTQ+ people)
OutdoorLads (Adventure activities for gay, bisexual and trans men)
Switchboard (LGBTQ+ mental health and wellbeing)
Non-Binary+ Northern Ireland (Support group / safe space for transgender and non-binary+ people)
Kamp Kiki (A retreat for trans people from the African and Caribbean diaspora)
Trans Bare All (Trans mental health and wellbeing)
BBZ Black Book (Online directory of queer women, trans and non-binary artists of Black ancestry)

LBGT Youth Scotland (Community-based organisation for LGBTQ+ youth)

FTM London (Support group for trans men / those who were assigned female at birth and are questioning their gender identity)

Exist Loudly (Creating space and community for queer Black youth)

Stonewall Housing (Housing for LGBTQ+ people)

African Rainbow Family (Support for LGBTQ+ people of African heritage and the wider Black Asian Minority Ethnic groups)

Trans Media Watch (Charity dedicated to improving media coverage of trans and intersex issues)

Beat For the GXDs (Online makeup creative space for Black non-binary and trans people)

Black LGBTQIA+ Therapy Fund (Therapy sessions for Black LGBTQ+ people)

HIDAYAH (Nationwide community group for LGBTQ+ Muslim people)

Sparkle (Raising awareness for the trans, non-binary/genderfluid and intersex community)

The Outside Project (LGBTQ+ homeless shelter)

Colours Youth Network (Creating space and community for young LGBTQ+ people of colour)

Bi Pride UK (Organisation supporting the UK's bisexual community)

Queer Futures (National study investigating LGBTQ+ suicide)

Imaan (Charity supporting LGBTQ+ Muslims)

Rainbow Noir (Support and community action group for LGBTQ+ people of colour)

Bi's of Colour (Support for those in the bisexual+ community who are Black and people of colour)

QTIPOC Brighton (Support for queer, trans, and intersex people of colour)

Persian LGBTQ (Support for LGBTQ+ asylum seekers and refugees)

UK Lesbian and Gay Immigration Group